Dave Hill was born in a castle in Devon and moved with his parents to Wolverhampton when he was a year old. As a teenager he taught himself to play guitar and in 1966 formed the band which would become Slade.

After the break-up of the original band, Dave eventually reformed Slade, and twenty-five years later, they are still regularly touring the world, playing to hundreds of thousands of fans. Dave married his wife Jan in 1973, and they have three children and five grandchildren. They still live in Wolverhampton.

SO HERE IT IS
THE AUTOBIOGRAPHY

DAVE HILL

Unbound

This edition first published in 2017

Unbound
6th Floor Mutual House, 70 Conduit Street, London W1S 2GF
www.unbound.com

Text Design by Ellipsis

A CIP record for this book is available from the British Library

ISBN 978-1-78352-420-4 (trade hbk)
ISBN 978-1-78352-421-1 (ebook)
ISBN 978-1-78352-422-8 (limited edition)

Printed in Great Britain by Clays Ltd, St Ives Plc

I dedicate this book in loving memory to my mom and dad, Jack and Dorothy

Dear Reader,

The book you are holding came about in a rather different way to most others. It was funded directly by readers through a new website: Unbound. Unbound is the creation of three writers. We started the company because we believed there had to be a better deal for both writers and readers. On the Unbound website, authors share the ideas for the books they want to write directly with readers. If enough of you support the book by pledging for it in advance, we produce a beautifully bound special subscribers' edition and distribute a regular edition and e-book wherever books are sold, in shops and online.

This new way of publishing is actually a very old idea (Samuel Johnson funded his dictionary this way). We're just using the internet to build each writer a network of patrons. At the back of this book, you'll find the names of all the people who made it happen.

Publishing in this way means readers are no longer just passive consumers of the books they buy, and authors are free to write the books they really want. They get a much fairer return too – half the profits their books generate, rather than a tiny percentage of the cover price.

If you're not yet a subscriber, we hope that you'll want to join our publishing revolution and have your name listed in one of our books in the future. To get you started, here is a £5 discount on your first pledge. Just visit unbound.com, make your pledge and type **slade5** in the promo code box when you check out.

Thank you for your support,

Dan, Justin and John
Founders, Unbound

CONTENTS

FOREWORD

I have known Mr Hill, or H, as we called him in the band, for well over fifty years, and worked with him in Slade for twenty-five years! He could be infuriating, zany, demanding and impatient, but also very funny, without even realising it. He is incredibly loyal, and protects the privacy of the Slade background and behaviour fiercely.

My first impression of Dave, all those years ago, was that he was very aloof. When eventually I got to know him properly, I found it was just that he did not follow the herd, he ploughed his own furrow and did his own thing. Nothing wrong with that! From day one any hilarious criticism about his eccentricity, his dress sense or his haircut was water off a duck's back. I totally empathised with his outlook. He was never going to be the one to fade into the shadows on stage, or on television.

When Dave asked me to join what was to become the new 'N Betweens, I don't think he'd ever seen me perform. It was drummer Don Powell and roadie Graham Swinnerton who were singing my praises to him. They'd seen my previous bands many times.

Dave did put his case very well. He wanted the new band to have a big colourful image, and that was right up my street. He wanted three lead guitar players, even on bass. He also wanted to get away from the straight blues format their band had been known for. All this suited me perfectly.

As far as I'm concerned Dave's biggest musical contribution to the band was his sound. It was always big, unsubtle and unique. Even from the old eclectic style of the 'N Betweens, through to what became the Slade guitar sound. All without the use of lots of effects pedals.

Since I left the band in 1991 we have not always seen eye to eye on some things. I'm afraid that's the nature of the beast in rock 'n' roll! But we have always respected one another and still manage to speak often. Dave has come down from 'Planet H' in the last few years and has got his priorities in life all sorted. We are now both in our seventies and we're still able to make each other laugh a lot, no mean feat... 'COZ I LUV YOU' Mr H.

Noddy Holder

SO HERE IT IS

You can all picture the scene, you've all been there. The little bedroom in your parents' house, all your gear in there, your clothes, your records, your coat hanging up on the back of the door. That was where I was still living at the age of twenty-six, not all that unusual in the 1970s, I suppose.

Only my story is a little bit different. I've got the number one record in the UK. Again. I'm in Slade, the biggest pop group in Britain, maybe Europe. I'm on the front cover of *Melody Maker*. I'm on *Top of the Pops* all the time. I've sprayed a halo of silver paint on that bedroom door around that coat – my dad's not best pleased with that! I've got my Jensen with the YOB1 plate parked in the road outside the house.

It's not all sweetness and light though. My mom is in hospital, the nut house as we called it. She's in and out of there a fair bit. My dad is devoted to her, and to me and my sister Carol, but Mom takes up a lot of his time. I suppose that meant we were left to our own devices a bit, that we could follow what we were interested in without anybody getting in the way, because Mom wasn't up to it and Dad was busy. Maybe that's why we both end up us as performers, looking for a bit of attention, not that I ever felt short of that!

In a lot of ways, that bedroom, that house sums up my story. For all the success I got, the places I went, the things I saw, it was never about escaping from home, which in my case was Wolverhampton. In fact, I'm still there now, pretty much a stone's throw from where I grew up – mind you, I wasn't bad at throwing stones as a kid!

It's not just a geographical thing. I don't think I've changed much from the kid who grew up on that council estate. For all the money and the fame that's come and gone and come again, I've still got the same values I had then. My family means the world to me – wife, kids, grandkids now, they're the foundation of everything.

And then there's the guitar. I still love picking it up, having a play, getting up in front of people and seeing them having a great time with all those songs. Fifty years and more since I first got on a stage, there's still no thrill like it when I walk on stage with Slade now, still me and Don Powell together after all we've been through.

Then there's my mom's depression, which has haunted me all my life, certainly later on. I don't know if it's genetic, if it was the fame and the life I led, or whether I just didn't fall very far from the tree, but I fell prey to the same problems later in my life and had to fight my way out of that. And then I had to get over a stroke that hit me while I was up there on stage.

It's been some journey, a lot of extremes. Life has taught me a lot on the way, mainly that you can't have everything at the same time! In the end, getting everything in balance is what really matters, that's what makes it all work out, and I think I've recently got closer to that than I ever did before, even when I was in that bedroom and on top of the music world.

Like I say, it's been some journey. So here it is...

1

BORN IN A CASTLE, RAISED IN A COUNCIL HOUSE

I was born in a castle in Devon, which, for a bloke who ended up being called Super Yob, isn't a bad start. It was in Flete, on a 500-acre estate owned by Lord Mildmay of Flete. During the war one of the local hospitals got bombed and so he gave over a wing of the building to be used as a maternity hospital. It carried on being used that way until 1958, and I came into the world there on 4 April 1946.

Why I was born there has always been a bit of a mystery, and the more I've dug into it, the more mysterious it's become. My parents had been living in the Potteries, which is where they'd met during the war when they were both working in a munitions works, Dad in the factory, Mom in the offices, all the result of strange circumstances that played a huge part in their lives and that of me and my sister.

My mom was from a fairly well-to-do background, very definitely middle class in the days when that meant something. She was born in 1913 and grew up in the roaring twenties, when being a cut above the workers counted for a lot. The family were pillars of the community. Her mother, Helen, was a teacher before she got married, and her father, David Bibby, was a well-educated man, a doctor of music who taught the subject. He was a very accomplished pianist and played the organ in the local church, so they were a significant family locally.

As my mom grew up, she became very attractive. She was intelligent, bright, acted in *The Mikado*, and was a dancer. She had it going on, as they say now. Unfortunately, that proved to be her downfall because she fell pregnant when she was just seventeen, and back in the 1930s that was a scandal, particularly for a middle-class family. As far as we know, she had a relationship with a married man, but on my half-sister Jean's birth certificate there's nobody down as the father. Over the years I've wondered if he was a prominent figure, perhaps somebody she worked for. Even at seventeen or eighteen, Mom was a very skilled secretary and would have caught a lot of people's eyes.

To escape the scandal, the family moved away. They ended up in the Potteries and settled in Newcastle-under-Lyme, but the upheaval nearly killed my grandmother, Helen. She was never right again after that because it was the kind of thing that brought shame and disgrace on the family in those days; it was an absolute taboo. She had a mental breakdown as a consequence and she went into a home and eventually died there.

While Helen was mortified, my grandfather David just accepted things. The situation was that he now had a granddaughter and he just got on with it. He found a companion for my mom, who we used to call Auntie Ethel, though she wasn't a relation, who acted as housekeeper for Granddad as well. Presumably, bringing up Jean was one of her tasks. We would visit her and her husband, Uncle Jack, a lot when we were kids.

That Jean was alive at all was a miracle because, as a lot of girls in that situation did at the time, Mom had tried to get rid of the baby – this was long before abortion was legal of course. She drank a bottle of gin, took some pills and threw herself down the stairs, but they both survived and Jean was born in 1931. This meant she was quite a bit older than me and Carol, who was born in 1949. By the time I was around and old enough to take any notice of what was going on, Jean was in her late teens, and the fact that she lived somewhere else never seemed strange. We just assumed she was our sister, had the same mom and dad, and nobody ever told us different.

While all of this was going on, Dad was growing up in the Potteries in a village called Barlaston, where he was the baker's son. Dad had a sense of adventure in him and when he was twenty, in 1923, he decided he was going to emigrate to Australia and went there on one of the government-sponsored schemes. I think it cost a fiver for your passage on the ship.

He had seven years out there, but because communications weren't like now, if you went to Australia, it was like you'd disappeared off the face of the earth. You couldn't really keep in touch with anybody other than by letters that took for ever to get back, and so in 1930 he came home, basically because he missed his mom. Take me bak 'ome...

When he got back, he was the star of the village. He'd been to Australia, which seemed unbelievable to the people in Barlaston, and he was also very dapper. He wore spats, Oxford bags, all very flamboyant, so it was no surprise that he attracted the ladies. Fairly soon, Dad got married to Cath, his sister Lilly's best friend. It didn't work out though because she was a ward sister in a hospital and didn't want children. Dad, on the other hand, was desperate to be a father. He said to us later that he wished he'd asked his wife before they got married if she wanted children because if he had, he'd never have gone through with it.

He then met my mom during the war in the munitions factory. She was working in the offices – we believe she'd been a cabinet minister's secretary at some point, though that was all very secret, but it may have been around that time. The factory was a prime target for German air raids. In that setting you didn't know if you were going to be alive the next day, so everything was very ramped up emotionally and they fell in love. They had their song, 'You'll Never Know', and things went from there. Dad told her that all he had ever wanted was to have children, and Mom told him, 'I'll have your children,' yet she didn't tell him about Jean, who was living with Auntie Ethel at this point. In fact, she didn't tell him for years; she kept it quiet and he only found out by confronting her when he felt something was wrong.

Dad told us that after we'd got our council house in Warstones, in Wolverhampton, Mom would regularly go out at night. One night he followed her because he thought she was having an affair. She went into a phone box – nobody had a phone at home then – and as she was dialling, Dad opened the door and demanded to know what was going on. That was when he found out about Jean – Mom was calling her. This was 1949, when I was already two or three years old, but this was the first he knew of it. And from there, he had a fantastic relationship with Jean.

So when Mom and Dad first met, she had already had a child; meanwhile, Dad's wife wouldn't let him have a divorce because there was an insurance policy involved and she wouldn't let Mom have the money. That didn't matter for a while – they could get round all of that – but when Mom fell pregnant with me, that was a different thing again. Piecing it all together now, I reckon that when that happened, they decided it was best if they scarpered to a different part of the country where nobody knew them. So poor Mom was on the run because of a baby again. But this was just after the war, when everything was being rebuilt, there were plenty of jobs, and Dad was a skilled mechanic, so it was easy for him to get work, which is how they ended up in Devon, presumably telling people down there that they were married.

They must have always intended to come back to the Midlands at some point though, because that's where their families were, but they still had this problem of not being married. So they worked up a way of getting round that – they mocked up a fake wedding at a register office! Incredible, and I only discovered that they did this quite recently. All their friends and family were left outside and they went in alone; none of the guests went in to see the ceremony. When they came out, Mom had a wedding ring on. I'd have thought that would have just made everybody suspicious, but either they turned a blind eye or people were a lot more trusting seventy years ago than they are now!

We never talked about birthdays or anniversaries at home and I do remember Carol got a bit fed up with it. When she was eleven or twelve, she said to Dad, 'Will you please tell me when your anniversary is so I can buy you a present?' And Dad said, 'Don't ask questions that you don't need to know the answer of.' We never knew until we were in our late teens or early twenties that they weren't married; we were just a family like everybody else.

After they'd pretended to get married, they were free to come back to the Midlands and Dad got a job in Wolverhampton. But there was a terrible housing shortage just after the war, so in the finish we lived in a two-up two-down with another family near Dunstall Park racecourse in Wolverhampton. We were there until I was around two.

During that time Mom and Dad both worked, and the people we were living with looked after me. Then one day Jean came in the house and found me screaming my head off in a room on my own. I don't know if that affected me in some way, but to this day I don't like being shut up in rooms. I like the light. I don't like to be enclosed, I like the open. I like to have control of my environment.

I'm sure the woman had only popped out to get something from the shops and thought I'd be fine on my own for a few minutes, but at that age you're not. I've always wondered if I've carried that through the years because I've always been a worrier, and possibly I also got some of this from how Mom was. Eventually I started having panic attacks, then I suffered from depression for a couple of years and had some very black times. I've always been very fearful about my health too. I remember when I was thirteen or fourteen I had a stomach problem and thought the worst. I went to see my headmaster and told him, 'I think I've got cancer, sir.' He just said, 'You don't get cancer at your age!' It was the best thing he ever said to me, because I believed him. I just believed him because he was older and so he would know. It was a trust thing.

I have always had the strong sense that if I do something wrong, something bad will happen to me as a consequence. I think that's something that has come down to me from my mom. As you can imagine, having Jean out of wedlock as a teenager really messed her life up. She was all set for a successful life and career – from a good family, a brilliant secretary, everything was set up for her – and then getting pregnant instantly took all that away. When you add in the fact that the family had to move and that her own mother had a breakdown and eventually died from the shock of it all, she was carrying a huge burden of guilt right from being a teenager.

I think she tried to transfer that guilt to others, simply because she couldn't handle it all herself. She came into my room one day, put my grandfather's doctor of music certificate on the wall and said to me, 'This is a good man,' and walked out. I was left trying to work out why I needed this example of a good man. Wasn't I good then? But that view of her father must have harked back to the pregnancy and the way he looked after her. I think she was incredibly grateful to him but also incredibly guilty because of the way her mother had taken it. She used that to make a point to me, and I'm sure that had an impact on me.

I don't feel any animosity towards her at all. I love my mom; she was just a victim of circumstances, of living in different times and moralities to the ones that followed. She had a lovely side to her, it wasn't all one way, but at heart she wasn't happy. Dad would come home from a long day at work and as soon as he walked through the door, she would hit him with problems, things I'd done or whatever. Then it would be, 'Don't hit him, Jack!' as if she felt guilty for telling him about me. Not that he ever did, just the very occasional clip round the ear that we all got in those days. Apart from the once, when I pocketed a watch that belonged to one of our relations, just a daft prank. He gave me a good hiding then, just to teach me a lesson.

You certainly wouldn't mess with Dad! When he went to Australia, as soon as he got off the boat somebody called him a Pommy, so he knocked him out! I never saw him hit anybody, but I'm sure he was capable of it. I was afraid of him, but only the way boys are of their dad. It was a healthy fear, the kind that kept you on the straight and narrow, because you didn't want to do anything so that you'd hear, 'Wait till your father gets home!'

Mom was also the kind of person who seemed to attract bad luck, and she couldn't handle it. After Jean was born for instance, Mom had a bad car accident and damaged her hip. The doctors told her that she couldn't have any more children, although that was disproved later with me and Carol!

Jean suffered from epilepsy, which again my mom saw as a punishment because she'd tried to end the pregnancy. Jean had terrible fits. I saw her have some of them. She'd fall flat on the floor and have convulsions. One time she was carrying a pan of boiling water and had a fit and poured it all down her body and she had to have skin grafts. Mom saw everything that went wrong as a punishment from God for what she saw as her wickedness in having a child out of wedlock. Her attitude was that bad things happen to bad people, which of course is nonsense. So if I did anything wrong, like when I chucked a brick through a window, that was her being punished.

It was a classic kid thing. I threw a brick at another kid who was messing around, missed and it smashed this window. The next thing I know, Mom's up in arms and I've been sent to bed to wait for Dad to come in and deal with it. Dad gets home and comes upstairs to find my mom in their bedroom with a scarf round her neck and a bottle of pills on the floor, looking like she's tried to kill herself, although she hadn't. He comes in and says, 'Get up, you silly bugger!'

Looking back on it, it seems to me that she was controlled by guilt, and anything that disturbed her life, however trivial it might have been, she saw as a punishment. It was like the world only existed to get her back. She didn't feel as if she could enjoy anything because she felt she didn't deserve it.

When we were young, after we'd moved to our council house on the Warstones estate, Carol was kidnapped. She was four at the time. Again, that was another chance for Mom to think she was being punished for her 'wickedness'.

It was a Sunday morning, and Carol was playing outside with a friend, Jackie Harrison. They'd got a pram and they were going round and round the cul-de-sac. Mom was doing Sunday lunch, Dad was watching them, and he went off for literally a minute to put his tie on, and when he came back, they'd gone. So he went round the other girl's house and shouted to them, 'Is our Carol in with you?' She wasn't and that was it, alarm bells were ringing.

Jackie had gone in, Carol had stayed outside and, in a flash, this woman had come into the cul-de-sac and taken her. She made her getaway with Carol on a bus, which is very Wolverhampton – there was nothing slick like a getaway car! The next thing Carol remembers is being found by another woman walking around in Wolverhampton town centre. She took her to the police, and Carol got brought home in a panda car, which she loved!

Life carried on and Mom had her ups and downs. Us kids, we didn't really notice much, but I've since found letters she sent to her sister when I was very young in which she says she wants to end it all, but that she couldn't because I'm around. It was clearly something buried very deep in her that only got worse as time went on.

A series of events in a short space of time in 1961 really took its toll on her. My mom was very friendly with our next-door neighbour, Mrs Malpas, a very earthy woman, and that was good for her because she didn't make friends easily. When Mrs Malpas was killed on the road I know it was a big blow to Mom.

Then there came a bigger loss. Jean, who had got married in 1953 when she was twenty-two, already had a son and had been told under no circumstances to have another child because of the epilepsy, but she became pregnant again. Towards the end of the pregnancy she was resting in bed and Ian, her son, came up wanting something to eat. He was only seven, so she got up to make him something. She went into the kitchen and presumably had a fit because she fell and banged her head on the cooker. She died the next day of a brain haemorrhage without regaining consciousness. The following morning Carol was at home in bed and Mom just walked into her room and said, 'Jean's dead,' very aggressive, quite nasty, and walked out.

I was away at the time, on holiday in Belgium with a couple of mates, the first time I had ever gone abroad, on a week's passport! A pokey little B & B we stayed in. On the ferry over one of the lads I was with, Keith Evans –

14

Evo – knocked my suitcase into the water! When I got home, it was to find the curtains drawn. The back door was always open so I went in and up to my bedroom because it was getting late. Dad came in and said, 'I've got some bad news.' That's how I found out.

Mom was blitzed by it. Somebody said to me years later that when we lost Jean, Mom died with her. The more I think about it, the more it feels like that might be right. Something switched off.

When she did go to work, it was better because she had other things to think about. She could get dressed up in her suit, go out and maybe she felt she was achieving something. But then she had a nasty accident. She always wore high heels, and this one day she slipped over when she was walking on lino and a jagged piece of it severed a tendon in her hand.

The doctor said to her, 'You'll never type again.' For Mom, that was it; all over. The idea that she would never again be able to work like she had – she was an incredibly fast typist, a very good secretary – was a terrible blow. It was the worst possible thing he could have said to her. That was the final straw after the loss of Jean and it threw her into a full-blown depression.

She was drinking as well, though she'd hide the booze, and that made her worse. She was on medication and then soon she was in hospital in Stafford, the nut house as we called it then. They took her there to have electric shock treatment. I was sixteen, seventeen, having to get time off from work to go and visit her, and the place was terrifying. I have very vivid memories of it and they are not pleasant. I used to go there on my Velocette motorbike, and I dreaded going in. You would walk down the corridor and hear screaming and crying, and at that age you really aren't prepared for that. It was still very Victorian.

I just couldn't wait to get out of there. It wasn't that I didn't love her, because I did, but I couldn't cope with the place. It was barbaric, and in those days nobody talked about mental illness because it wasn't the done thing. You went and then you came away and you kept it to yourself.

Years later, in 1975, Slade all went to see *One Flew Over the Cuckoo's Nest* at the pictures together. The other three were laughing, but I wasn't amused at all; it was too close to the bone. As soon as it started, I could just see Mom and Stafford. I found it insulting.

Dad was fantastic through it all. He used to go and visit her in Stafford every day, and the nurses used to say that nobody else did that for their wife or husband in there. He just loved her. I think he felt a bit guilty as well – that he'd failed her by bringing her to a council house in Wolverhampton after the way she'd been brought up and what she was used to.

But through everything Dad never let it affect him. When she died, despite all the problems and the things he'd had to deal with – caring for her later on, all of that – he told me that he really did miss her, and I don't think he was ever the same again.

It was dramatic what the electric shock treatment did. She came out of Stafford and sat at home, and for a little while she was almost normal, asking sensible questions, but it wouldn't last. After a while she'd be a mental wreck again and would end up back there. One time she went out and we realised we didn't know where she was. Then there was a knock at the door and one of the neighbours was outside. 'I've brought your mom home – I found her on the floor in the street.' Mom was standing there, smiling, with blood pouring out of her hand where she'd broken her thumb, the bone sticking out of the skin.

Another time, Carol came in from work and was in a hurry to go out, so as she went upstairs to get ready, she called, 'Mom, is dinner ready?' She came down ten minutes later and there were two raw lamb chops on a plate. She said, 'Is that it?' Mom said, 'You can eat it!' So Carol had a strop and said, 'Oh, forget it!' Mom picked up a steak knife and went for her with it, screaming. Thank God, Dad came in at just that minute, saw what was going on, smacked her hand, and the knife went flying through the air and straight into the fish tank! Carol was always terrified after that that Mom might try and stab her when she was in bed.

The thing was, it wasn't really Mom then. The person she was had gone. It was 1976 when she died. She saw me become famous, but Dad was the one who came to the gigs, he always saw us when we played the Civic Hall. I don't remember my mom ever coming to see Slade live. She was always ill.

We took her to the premiere of the Slade film *Flame* in Wolverhampton, and there's a photograph in the *Express & Star*, but she didn't look good. There was a whole physical change in Mom when she became ill, and before she died I remember Dad saying to me, 'I looked at her one day and I could see straight through her,' like he was looking at a ghost. I think he was trying to tell me she wouldn't be here much longer.

I got a phone call. Dad said, 'Your mom's died.' I can't remember crying or anything, it was just *Mom's died*. So I went over and he was sitting downstairs. He said, 'I didn't know till the morning.' He had felt her and she was freezing cold. She had died in the night. He asked if I wanted to see her but I couldn't face it. I didn't want to look at her.

My wife, Jan, has said to me a lot of times over the years that I never mourned my mom's death, and she's right. There were no tears. It was as though we'd lost her a long time before that. She was just existing. In a way, her death finally set her free from that guilt.

2

GROWING UP IN WOLVERHAMPTON

My real memories start when I was growing up in our council house in Rindleford Avenue, on the Warstones estate in Penn, just outside Wolverhampton. Being in our kitchen meant batteries, carburettors and the smell of petrol to me because when Dad was fixing stuff, he'd bring it in there to work on. Then there was the big tub they'd use to wash the clothes in. Mom would be trying to cook in there as well, so she was always saying, 'You can't swing a ruddy cat in here!'

Saying that, the place was very cleverly designed – they'd worked out the way council houses needed to operate. There was a walk-in pantry where all the food was kept – no fridges – then you had the coal hole outside the back door. It seemed very advanced because we'd got an indoor toilet, which made it feel like a brave new world, but if you fancied a bit of nostalgia, there was an outdoor toilet by the coal hole as well!

When we moved in, the estate was still being built, it

was a building site really, cement mixers everywhere, the gardens weren't done. But it was the start of something, a new era after the war. People were getting new houses. It was a very hopeful time, I do remember that as I was growing up.

My room was freezing, and I still don't like a hot bedroom. My bed had a dip in the middle – it had the same mattress for years and years – so I couldn't fall out of bed. I have wonderful memories of Christmas there. The windows used to get frozen up on the inside. It was like a scene from *Doctor Zhivago* – the street lights coming through the bedroom because I was at the front.

Both my parents worked when I was young. Mom was clever and got dressed up to go to work, a sharp, well-cut suit. She earned enough for us to have a few extras like holidays, because Dad's wages wouldn't have stretched to that kind of thing. He was working as a mechanic, and he'd come home at night in his boiler suit and plunge his hands in a tub of Swarfega to get them clean. I can still remember the stink of that stuff now. Because they worked, me and Carol were latchkey kids. Mom and Dad weren't at home when we finished school, so we had somebody look after us until they got back.

Dad was bright and he'd wanted to set up his own garage at one time along with another bloke, but because he had a steady job at a garage at the time, that never came off. My mom wasn't well with her depression on and off, not that I really knew about any of that, so he had to provide for the family and bring stability, and it was too big a risk for him to take.

It was a posh garage that he worked at, Castlecroft, at a time when normal working people didn't have cars. We certainly didn't have one, but we were lucky because he could use the garage car. When he took me down there, it was like going in a toyshop, being able to jump in all these big cars, all of them black in my memory.

Sometimes he'd bring the van home and occasionally he'd let me sit in it and start the engine up. 'But don't you put it in gear!' So of course I did, and the one day there was a milk float behind, which I hadn't seen, and I was going back slowly and reversed into the side of it. Dad came out and blamed the milkman for not getting out of the way!

On a Saturday they'd contract him out to B. C. Barton in Tipton, where he fixed American forklift trucks, and because my mom was at work I'd go with him. The trucks were expensive to repair because you had to get the parts in from America, but Dad was clever enough to make some of the parts himself and he saved them a fortune. Then on a Sunday you'd get neighbours knocking on the door and asking him to fix something. 'What the bloody hell do you want? It's me day off!' But after he'd had his whinge, he'd go out and sort it out for them.

My mom was a bit like that as well, because she'd teach the local girls to do Pitman shorthand. Or if somebody needed an official letter doing, she'd help them with that. A lot of our neighbours didn't know how to use a telephone, so she would make calls on their behalf because she was familiar with that world. She'd worked as a top secretary at some serious companies and it was through her connections that she got me my first proper job, at Tarmac, where I'd have to phone her up at the building company she was working at to order bricks!

Mom was a middle-class woman who'd ended up living a working-class life in a council house. Looking at pictures of her as a young girl with her family – in a park, there's a car behind them, they're having a tea party – it's a world away from the Warstones estate. She'd come down in the world socially, and I think she had a real chip on her shoulder about that. She wanted a better house and all that went with it.

I never had any feelings like that. I loved our estate. It was very friendly, we were all in it together. If anybody was ill, you all rallied round, people would fetch other people's washing in if it rained, you knew everybody's business. It was that wartime spirit carried into the post-war world, I suppose, a real sense of community. There wasn't much money about, so that community spirit was massively important, everybody looked after one another. It's a bit of a cliché now, but you genuinely did leave the door unlocked, you never even thought about it.

It was a great place to grow up. We were four miles from Wolverhampton but also in the country, the middle of nowhere yet a place where you seemed to have everything around you – shops, countryside, town, villages. My mom and dad would take me for a walk near where we lived, down a place called Dirty Foot Lane, which I wrote a song about many years later. I suppose we've all got a place like that from our childhood where we walked or played or rode our bikes. Later on I'd go there with friends like Tony. We would go into the fields over Orton Hill – lots of places to play in, you could get up to all sorts of things!

I remember me and a friend, Roger, we used to go into this one shop some mornings. Roger knew the bloke behind the counter, Vic, because he used to wash his car. We'd go in and Roger would say, 'Is that the phone ringing in the back, Vic?' When he went to check, we'd lean over the counter and pinch a Mars Bar! Then there was a big old house down the road where the milkman used to leave the milk in the morning, so I'd nip in the garden and guzzle it down before they came out to get it!

It all felt very safe, we'd go and play and nobody was ever concerned about anything happening to you. I never felt bored and I never had any desire to run away to the big city. I always felt at home there. Years later, I'd take my kids to the same places because we still lived within a few minutes of where I grew up.

As kids, you'd run errands. I remember going to the off-licence round the back of the pub, and I'd get Mom a bottle of Double Diamond and I'd have a Vimto. I'd get up to daft things as well, like kids do. Dad was a crack shot and he had a rifle from the war. Just before the Ministry of Defence had them back in, he had it in his bedroom with a box of live ammunition. One day I decided to get the bullets out and I started burying them in the garden, but I gave one to a kid who lived over the road. He thought it was a dummy and for some reason chucked it in the boiler at home and it exploded!

There was a bloke in the cul-de-sac called Alan who used to wear a tweed jacket with string around it. He was usually half-cut. The one day we were outside and he said to me and Carol, 'You tie me up, and if I can't get free, you win sixpence.' He was drunk and we really got him, he couldn't get out of it and he didn't like it! I'd got my hands in his pockets trying to find the sixpence; he was screaming and shouting.

Being a bit posh, my mom's side of the family had an artistic bent. Maybe she saw some of that in me, because when I was nine or ten she wrote a letter to the school to try and get me involved in the violin and recorder class, which I didn't really fancy, but she saw it as a way of finding out if I had any musical ability.

The headmistress, Mrs Friar, who we called Friar Tuck of course, she got the hump with this letter. Teachers didn't like being questioned by mere parents! She said, 'You can't be in the musical group because you can't read music, boy.' It was a real put-down. I didn't even get an opportunity, she just stubbed me out right away, and I remember feeling very strange about that at the time, that there was something that I was being stopped from doing.

I got my revenge on the education system years later though. Me and Tony used to mess around a bit, and the one night we broke into my old school. We were just mucking about when suddenly the caretaker arrived on the scene and we legged it. Little did we know that around the same time somebody else had broken in as well and carved up one of the teachers' desks, so now we were the prime suspects.

About a week later I got dragged in for an interview at my senior school. The police were there with the headmaster, who looked like Charlie Chaplin with his little moustache, sitting there with his cape on.

'There's been an incident at your old school and we understand that you may know something about it?'

I just lied. I made up a story about seeing a chap with crew-cut hair. But what I didn't know was that they were going to interview Tony separately, and he told them the truth, so now Hill was a liar. Even worse, I went home at lunchtime to feed Taffy the dog and there was a police car parked outside our house. The driver rolled the window down and said, 'We know the truth. Tony has told us everything. Tell your mom and dad we're coming round to see you tonight.'

So that night I had to go home and tell Mom and Dad that the police were coming round the house. I remember sitting at the table, having my tea, thinking, *How am I going to tell them what's happening?*

So I said, 'I sneaked into my old school last night.'

'What do you mean, sneaked in?'

So I told them what had happened and I said, 'The detectives saw me at school and they're coming round later.'

That was it, Mom was alive to all of it. 'Detectives? Interviewing you on your own? You're under age, they can't do that!' She put in an official complaint, and now this headmaster who fancied himself for getting a new job at a posh grammar school might lose the one he's got because he's allowed this to happen.

Not only that, my mom knew the top policeman at the local station, so she got on the phone to him because the police were in the wrong as well and it would have been a scandal. So it all went very quiet and through the following week the headmaster would keep fetching me out of class and marching me to his office, 'What's your mom doing now? What's she going to do?'

A couple of weeks later, we were all called up to Red Lion Street, the police station, and before we went, Mom said, 'It's all fixed, just go along with it.' So we're there – me, Tony, our parents – and this copper says, 'Are we going to see a repeat of this?' So we say no and that's it! It was removed from the records and it was all over. If it hadn't been for Mom, who knows what might have happened?

That was her at her best, when she had it all together. She was like that several times. Dad had a very bad accident underneath a car at work and he lost an eye. He was knocking away at something and a little chip of metal went right through the pupil. Because of the way things were in those days the delay between getting him to hospital and having him seen to was enormous. I guess it could have been saved but it wasn't.

It was an accident at work. What did that mean? Mom knew. She started a fight to get him a lump sum of insurance money. I remember the day of the case. He didn't win because he wasn't wearing protective glasses. These were the days of guys lying on their backs underneath cars, real mechanics, no thought about protective gear or health and safety. Mom knew Enoch

Powell personally and got him involved. He was the MP yet she could talk to him and he was a tough cookie. She carried a bit of weight with these people.

She fought the eye thing, and though Dad didn't get a lump sum, they offered him a pension plan and paid him a special allowance every month. I think he got that until the day he retired because he carried on working, although the accident left him with split vision. He also got migraine headaches and he had to go to a specialist. Typical Dad though, he turned having a glass eye into something funny. He would get it out and show my mates, and there was a bit of a queue to see it. He was a little bit of a showman and nobody had ever seen somebody pull their eye out! One lad came in the house and Dad had forgotten that he had left his eye in the sink upstairs. The kid went in the bathroom, and the eye was looking at him and this kid flipped his lid, he ran down the stairs and out of the front door. He thought it was alive!

As a kid I always responded to music. We had a little wind-up gramophone, and sometimes I'd take it out the front on the grass and play it. We had this record 'Lollipop' and I'd play it really loud, just to annoy the neighbours. 'David Hill, shut that row up!' We didn't have many records, though my dad was quite into classical music. I couldn't afford to buy many, but you'd get these cheap pop records from Woolworths, on the Embassy label, cover versions of the proper records from America. There was a kid at school who actually had a record collection. You had to go round his house to see it, they were too precious to lend to anybody!

When I moved on to senior school, a kid down the road, Ray Bates, got a guitar. It was just an acoustic – nobody had seen an electric one at that time – but it looked great and I fancied a go, so I went and told my dad. 'If you want to do it, you'll need lessons. We'll give it a go. You'll have to put half of your paper round money in. I'll pay the rest and I'll buy you the guitar.'

That was very much his philosophy on life. You don't get given things, you go and earn them, and that was what he was teaching me then, and it was a lesson that stayed with me. He was very much about doing what you had to do in life, standing on your own two feet. I remember my first day at infant school, Mom and Dad standing at the gate. I was walking in crying. I remember looking round at them. She was going, 'Jack, shall I fetch him back?' and Dad said, 'No, he has got to go.'

He was very encouraging, very positive, though years later, when I was still living in the box room at home when Slade were having number ones, he was a bit less encouraging when I hung one of my stage costumes up on the back of a door to spray it with silver paint and glitter, and then when I took it off, the door was covered in the stuff. He wasn't so keen on that!

But otherwise he was very positive, so much so that later on in the 1970s Dad bought me a very special guitar from London, a Gibson. I had a red Burns guitar at the time and Chas Chandler wasn't happy with it, he wanted me to get something better. The Gibson was £220 – more than forty years ago – and Dad shelled out on it. It was a big investment, but that was Dad. Once he knew I was committed to something, he'd go out of his way to help and encourage me.

Anyway, back at the start of it all, I got the Kay's catalogue out and started looking through it, and I just got this weird sensation from looking at the guitars. It was all really exotic at the time because there were no guitar shops round where I lived. There was a music shop in Wolverhampton selling flutes and violins, but nothing with guitars. And there were all kinds, these big things with the 'f' holes that Wes Montgomery used, all kinds of prices, but my dad didn't want to spend too much in case I didn't take to it.

If you had something out of the catalogue, you'd pay so much a week, spreading the cost. The guitar I got cost seven pounds ten shillings, a fortune, but it was a dreadful thing. It arrived in a cardboard box. I got it out, had no idea how to hold it, which was made more complicated by me being left-handed. Then off I went for lessons with this guy who was a jazz guitarist but who taught on the side. As soon as he saw it, he said, 'You'll never get anywhere with a guitar like that!'

It would never happen now, but he made me learn right-handed, and I think that was actually good for me because it's my stronger left hand that plays the frets, that's where the power and the feel is. My right is the rhythm hand, which is probably the more straightforward part. Because of that, I developed the David Wobble. Because I am left-handed but play guitar right-handed, I back-bend strings. I push them down. Others push them up. I wobble the note, I pull it. That is a lot to do with how I play chords and things like that. We have some quirky chords in Slade songs. With me it is about striking, timing and a sharpness. It has power but it is rhythmic as well. You get something like AC/DC where they are strident on their chords, quite cutting. I am more of a melodic guitarist but I am quite powerful. When I hit it, I hit it! I've got a friend who's left-handed and learned that way and he wishes he hadn't; he reckons I've got an advantage.

In fairness, there were no such things as left-handed guitars then, except maybe in Denmark Street in London, who knew? Paul McCartney hadn't appeared on the scene playing left-handed yet, so nobody really thought about the idea very much. You just got on with it. I had a few lessons, not many though, and then I went on from there by myself.

I remember buying sheet music for 'Tell Laura I Love Her' and learning that in my mom's bedroom, strumming away with this lad Ray from down the road, who was a bit more advanced than me and told me, 'Yo'm playing that wrong!' He had a Grundig tape recorder as well so we could listen back to ourselves. It was quite advanced because there was a superimpose button on it, so you could record another bit on top of what you already had, a rudimentary kind of double-tracking which was pretty futuristic.

I kept playing, I got a bit better, and I had to move on from that ropey acoustic, so I got an electric guitar. There was a group who performed at the youth centre and they had electric guitars, so that was it then, that was what I wanted to do.

The Shadows were also starting to come through then, and that changed things because before that it was all Lonnie Donegan, skiffle, tea-chest bass and washboards, all acoustic. I got on stage with one of those bands at the cinema on a Saturday morning after the films had finished, just a few of us kids making a noise really, and I was up there, eyeing up a blonde down the front. The idea of being up on stage and showing off struck a chord in me then, and it's been with me ever since.

Once the Shadows had plugged in, that was something completely different, it changed things. This was the first homegrown rock 'n' roll sound, not just the stuff we'd heard from America like Elvis or Buddy Holly. I vividly remember seeing Cliff Richard for the first time on television, he was on *Oh Boy!* – this would be around 1961. He came on, looking a bit like Elvis, wearing this striped shirt, flipped up collar, hair combed back. He definitely had the look, and you couldn't forget it once you'd seen him. 'My God, who's this bloke?' He hadn't got the Shadows with him at the time, but they quickly joined forces, and that started the big change. But I never had any thoughts of being a rock star, even though everybody always thinks I just wanted to be the centre of attention. I was just fascinated by trying to work out how to play guitar.

It was all very naive. You couldn't watch a DVD to learn how to do it; there was no YouTube; the only instruction book I'd ever heard of was Burt Weedon's

Play in a Day, though I never got it. All we'd got was the radiogram or the Dansette record player, and you just listened and listened to these records and tried to work it out and copy them.

I remember the excitement, the buzz I got from learning something like 'Theme For Young Lovers' by the Shadows. I'd play a bit, then lift the needle up and try and play it, then drop the needle again. There was no rewinding a tape or anything, so it took ages. The great thing with the Shadows was that the melodies were so intuitive, I learned those first in my bedroom, before working out the chords.

Dad was very encouraging with the guitar – he wanted me to have something that was mine. He was very practical, very clever and in later years worked out how to plug my guitar into the radiogram that we had, which was like an early music centre, a radio and a record player in a cabinet. He figured out that it had an amplifier and sorted it out so that I could plug my guitar into it.

Mom didn't say much about the guitar but obviously heard me playing in the house. I remember her sitting and listening to me and drifting off and, thinking about it later, I think it reminded her of her father, David Bibby, who was a very gifted player. He's where I got my name from. He was a music teacher, a concert pianist and a bit of an entertainer too because by all accounts every now and again he'd go to the working men's club and play piano and they'd buy him drinks, which was a bit daring for the times, so there was that performing streak in the family even going back to then. I remember a bit later on playing 'Born To Be Wild', and she said, 'I really like that.' That was a different side to my mom!

We'd started a group on the estate by now. John Bradford was our singer. I'd known him for years because when we were latchkey kids, me and Carol would go and stop at his house until Mom came to get us. When he heard I had a guitar, he knocked on our door and said, 'You looking for a singer?' I hadn't thought about it to be honest, but why not? He was a bit of a Tom Jones type. So we formed a group with Tony, who had gone and bought a bass when I started messing about with the guitar.

We got this amplifier and I took it round Tony's house. He'd got his bass and I had my guitar and we were going to plug the pair of them into it, but it didn't have a mains plug. So he said, 'I'll put it on the light fitting.' So he goes up and undoes the light fitting and sticks the bare wires straight into it. He could have blown the house up!

Then there was a lad called Keith Evans – Evo – who looked a bit like Cliff. He was very confident and we thought he'd be good to have in the group – I thought he'd make a good singer because of how he looked – but we already had John, so Evo decided to get a drum kit. I turned up at his house one day and he'd got himself a snare drum. Nothing thought out really. It all just fell together, just something to do.

We played at the Victory Hall in the village, we'd been offered half a crown – two shillings and sixpence – so we weren't turning that down! There was just the three of us on this stage, me, Tony and Evo. John wasn't there, and the stage seemed pretty big. We got dressed up, we each put a cummerbund on so we looked different, and then walked on the stage and played 'FBI'. And people started bopping! I remember being up there and looking at them and thinking, *This is all right!* I was amazed.

We started getting some songs together. A lot of it was Shadows stuff, and John introduced me to Chuck Berry. He was into American music, 'Johnny B. Goode', all that kind of thing. This was another world opening up. What they called the barre chord was a big part of that, very much a part of the blues world. It's a rhythmic way of playing a chord, and you'd use it to change the tone. You'd have a finger across the guitar to hold down all the strings and then use the other fingers to form a chord, where before it was more open and more country and western in sound, that typical skiffle thing. It gave the sound a definite edge, a real change.

We had various names that we went under. We were the Young Ones, we were the Shamrocks, I think, then it was the Sundowners after an old Western film, which is what we eventually settled on. It was the typical thing of kids in groups – the members would change, and one day Evo upped and joined another band. He ended up in a group called the Californians. They used to all wear white, very much like the Beach Boys, and they ended up touring with Jimi Hendrix, Cat Stevens and the Walker Brothers.

Evo leaving wasn't really a big deal. We weren't really that serious at the time – we were only rehearsing at the youth centre and weren't playing many shows. We'd meet and learn a new tune every Sunday, but hardly ever played anywhere. Everything used to go on at the youth centre. I remember walking there with my guitar in one hand and the amp in the other.

A mate of John's, Stewart Wilkes, came on the scene then and said he was going to be our manager. He was a builder but promised to get us some shows. He was good as his word and suddenly we were a real band. We played a few local pubs, that kind of thing. Our first gig, when Evo was still with us, was at the Percy Thomas Hall in Wolverhampton, which later became the Lafayette.

While this was all starting out, I was working at Tarmac. I left school at fifteen, as a lot of kids did then, and went into this office job that Mom had sorted out for me, which got right in the way of things! It did come in handy the once though, because I was struggling to get the middle part of 'FBI' right and I was talking about it to a woman at work who said, 'My husband's in a band called the Ramrods. They rehearse in Bilston. Go and see him because I think he knows how to play that.'

I went across to the Toc H in Bilston and they were playing upstairs. As I walked in, it was one of those moments that live with you for ever. I loved the echo sound that Hank Marvin used on his records. I knew he used an echo chamber to get the sound. He played muted notes which repeated through the chamber and built up this big sound that became his trademark. Joe Brown had given it to him because he couldn't work out what to do with it. And as I walked in this room in Bilston, I could hear the chattering of an echo chamber. It's a tape device, and as it goes round it ratchets and clicks where there's the join in the tape.

It turned out it belonged to Lenny Beddows, who was the guitar player that I'd come to talk to. He played 'FBI' and it sounded like the bloody record! He taught me the bit that I couldn't work out, and I was delighted. We could go and put that in our act.

There were a lot of bands around locally, everybody was forming a group at the time. John knew a guy called Mack Woolley who was a drummer. Mack was a bit of an entertainer, he'd turn up in a Beatles wig one week, the next he'd be something else, one of those blokes who's always formulating big ideas, none of which ever happens. He was looking for some musicians, and me and John went to play in this band. They were doing stuff like 'Reet Petite', older songs – they were older blokes as well – so I was a bit of a misfit. I didn't really enjoy it, but I went along for the ride.

One night we played a pub and in the audience was a bloke called Chalky White. I think he spotted that I was in the wrong band, a kid with these older geezers. The next day he turned up at our house and said, 'Are you interested in joining a group in Bilston that I manage called the Vendors?' I was living in Penn, and this bloke wants me to go to Bilston, which is at least five or ten miles away? We couldn't even understand what they said in Bilston, it was that far off. It's funny how insular we were then. You never went anywhere. Dudley, about ten miles away, was like the moon. I remember a bit later we played in a pub on an estate there, the Wren's Nest.

Sound nice? It wasn't! It was really rough, and it wasn't the blokes, it was the girls fighting in front of us!

Anyway, Chalky says, 'We're looking for a lead guitarist, and I saw you last night and I think you'd fit in. If you're interested, I can take you over now, just bring your guitar.'

I went off to meet them at the singer's house, and they were really friendly, all this ''Ow om ya me mon?' I couldn't understand a word. I was working at Tarmac, I was a bit posh! The drummer hadn't said a word though. He went and sat at the kit, and they asked me what I knew. So I said, 'What about "Johnny B. Goode"?' because I knew I could bring this barre chord out and impress everybody. Afterwards the drummer just looked at me in amazement – he'd never seen anybody play like that before. I played a bit of lead guitar as well and they were all gobsmacked apparently. I'd got the job.

So I went back home and I didn't know what to do because I'm really loyal with people. John Bradford was my singer, we'd gone through bands together, and I felt like I was leaving him behind. So I told him that I'd been offered this job but I said, 'I'm only taking it if they put you in the group as well.'

So he came with me to see them and we played 'Come On' by the Stones. We'd started, and I thought that Mick Marston, the rhythm player, was playing the wrong chords. 'Mick, you should change on that chord.'

'I like it like this.'

'OK, Mick.'

That was it, conversation over. He wasn't changing anything!

Worse than that, we were trying to fit two singers in now with John Bradford, but their singer, John Howells, was really good, a proper soul singer.

To make it more complicated, we were still in the group with Mack, so we needed to rehearse with them. I went to the next rehearsal, but when I arrived there was another lead guitarist already there playing with them! Mack came over, put his arm round me and said, 'Don't take it to heart, Dave. You'll be better off in another group anyway.' John Bradford ended up staying with them and I left. I suppose it made life simpler in the end.

That was life-changing as it turned out. The Vendors played our first gig together on 3 January 1964. Beatlemania had happened, the Stones were getting famous, there was the blues explosion, you could start to see possibilities in all this. And the Vendors, they were different to any band I'd been in before. I wouldn't say they were especially good – I was probably more advanced as a player at that point, more experienced as a musician – but the way they acted around each other was different. They were mates, they all used to stop round each other's houses. I wasn't used to that, it was new to me. They were like a gang and I was really getting into it.

At the same time, at Tarmac I was starting to get a bit of resistance to it all. 'You don't want to be messing about with groups, it's just a fad. You've got a proper job here.' As a group, we were looking a bit casual like the Stones. We were growing our hair, I was experimenting with a fringe because of the Beatles, though I had to comb it back when I went home because my mom didn't like it!

I have always had big ears and I had a complex about them, and I used to do something really silly. I used to tie one of dad's ties across my forehead to pin my ears flat against my head, and leave it there overnight, hoping that my ears would go flat. Dad came down one morning and bawled at me, 'You'll strangle yourself if that tie gets caught on the bedpost!' He asked what I was doing and I was embarrassed to tell him, but everyone was combing their hair forward, and of course if you have big ears, they stick out. This was before the Beatles grew their hair over their ears. So the Beatles were a great help to me in a lot of ways. It wasn't the hairstyle that I would have when I became famous, but it was a start.

There was a lot of tension between the various parts of my life at that time. The Vendors were getting more work, especially after we became the 'N Betweens in November 1964. Meanwhile I was going to night school from Tarmac, but I was eighteen and really getting into the band. I'd moved on with my playing, I wasn't much bothered about night school. I really enjoyed being with the blokes in the group, I liked that environment. We were meeting for rehearsals at a Scout hut in Bilston, and Dad would sometimes ferry the gear round for us in a black Daimler – he put a little flag on the front with the band's name on it! Dad would stop and listen while he had a cigar. I played him 'Theme For Young Lovers', and he said, 'That was pretty good, son. Not as good as Hank, but pretty good!'

I'd take my stage clothes into work with me in a plastic bag and hide them in my desk, and the one night the band turned up in a van – what we called the Passion Wagon – to collect me to do a show. The personnel department got wind that I was in a group, not doing well at night school and not concentrating on my job. I was terrible at spelling so I'd be filing records in the wrong place and they wouldn't be able to find them again. I got called in and was given a lecture.

We'd just had an offer to go to Germany, to Dortmund, for a month. We'd played an audition at Le Metro in Birmingham, a lot of bands trying out in front of these club owners. They liked us and offered us a month out there, November 1965, but to do that we had to turn professional, chuck in our jobs. It was funny how I found out about it. I was in night school and I looked up at these faces pressed up against the window. It was the band. 'We've got the job!'

So I went home to my mom and dad and told them that the personnel officer had told me to shape up or I'd lose my job, but I wanted to pack it up and give this group thing a try. I laid it on thick that the Beatles had been to Germany before they made it, but to be truthful they didn't need much convincing.

Dad especially was all for it. 'But keep your night school going, David, so you've got something to fall back on.' That lasted five minutes! I remember trying to do my homework on a Saturday morning with the radio on,

Brian Matthew, *Saturday Club*. I'd be doing technical drawing, which I hated, and he was chatting to Paul McCartney on the phone from America.

Surprisingly, it wasn't a drama at home. I think because of her background, for my mom the idea of being in the arts wasn't outlandish. If she'd come from a more working-class background, she'd have probably gone mad at the idea of me chucking in a proper job.

Dad said to me, 'Some people have to work at a thing and others have got it in them. You've got this in you.' I also think he felt that he hadn't pursued his ambitions and maybe regretted that, and so he wanted me to give it a go.

So that was it. I chucked my job in and turned professional as a guitarist. I grew my hair and started to spend more and more time with the band, which was great. By now even the drummer was talking to me.

His name was Don Powell.

3

THE 'N BETWEENS

Through 1965, as The 'N Betweens, we'd been spending more and more time playing together and starting to develop what we were as a group. The exciting thing was that as we were doing it, Britain – and the British music scene – was changing massively too. I'd grown up in post-war Britain, and through the 1950s everything was still in black and white. You got Cliff going off on his *Summer Holiday*, but that was it. If you wanted colour, you had to look to the Americans, and they dominated, especially Elvis Presley.

Elvis was just mind-blowing, the way he looked and the way he performed, gyrating around, which he had got off the black guys in the R & B scene. Elvis would wear glitzy jackets too. There's the famous picture of him in a gold suit, so I wasn't the first one to wear something satiny, silky or glitzy!

That music started coming over here, and as I've said, Hank Marvin had a huge impact on me. Guitarists like Eric Clapton, Keith Richards, Jimmy Page, Jeff Beck, people a couple of years older than me, were listening to a lot of blues records, but for me it was a more modern sound, the echo sound. Maybe I had more of a sweet tooth musically, though I did like Chuck Berry, and it was that sweet sound I brought to the 'N Betweens.

In the 'N Betweens we did learn some blues stuff – probably via the Rolling Stones because that was going on in the charts – but it was never a big part of what we did because Don hated it. He thought it was really boring for a drummer; he was much more interested in Motown things. But we had a listen to John Lee Hooker and Sonny Boy Williamson. Those names cropped up, but it all sounded like the roots of the American Great Depression. It didn't mean much to us in Wolverhampton, it didn't really connect. We wanted a good time, something to take us away from how drab life was in those days. Britain was still like a country in wartime, it hadn't moved on much in the 1950s, especially where we were from. I suppose we were getting blues music one step removed, getting Elvis's version of it, a bit sweeter. The music that most affected me then, same as now, was really great songs. I was into it for that, not as a soloist the way Beck or Clapton were. I hadn't got much money, so I wasn't an avid record buyer the way some of those guys were. I didn't go hunting for obscure records so much, I was happy with what was popular as we moved on to the 45s after the big old 78s.

As the band played more gigs, like every band does we needed more material to play, and that was when we branched out a bit and went out as far as Birmingham. There was a shop there called the Diskery, and you could take piles of records into the booths and play them, and we'd listen to see if we could use them. It was all American stuff, soul and R & B.

It was the Beatles that really started to change things in this country. They were a revelation. This was the future, and without turning it into a cliché, it was like film in Britain had gone from black and white to colour – when *Help!* came out in Technicolor in July 1965, that was the signal that things really had changed here. For me that was when working in Tarmac got too restricting and I really wanted to go off and grow my hair, get rid of my tie, play my music.

We were lucky that the month in Dortmund fell into our laps when it did, because that forced our hand. So off we went: me, Don on drums, Mick Marston on guitar, Dave Jones, who we called Cass, on bass and John Howells singing. We were a good little unit that had been together for about a year as the 'N Betweens by then, though me, Don, John and Mick had been playing together as far back as January 1964.

Heading over there in November '65, it was a proper adventure. We got on the ferry to Ostend, then drove overnight to Dortmund. This is only three years after the Beatles had done all their stuff in Hamburg remember, so it felt like we were following in their footsteps. In fact, people used to say I looked a bit like George Harrison then, and there was this girl on the ferry who fancied me. I enjoyed playing that up with the rest of the lads, but I never saw her again!

It was a long drive, right through the night, and we

eventually got to Dortmund and parked outside the club at about six in the morning. The club was shut of course, and we were shattered, but this bloke looking like a farmer rolled up. We told him we were the band and asked what were we supposed to do now.

He told us we were staying at a farmhouse a few miles away on the outskirts of the city. The people who owned the club also had one in a town called Witten, and there was another English band playing there and we were both staying at the farmhouse. There were the five of us sleeping in the one room, and we were there for a month. The other band was just across the corridor. We had military-style metal beds with a dirty great pipe off a stove to keep the room warm because it was freezing cold – just like you see in the Colditz films! I didn't care. This was freedom. No more being told what to do at school or at Tarmac, and fourteen pounds a week!

Because of the part Hamburg had played in the story of the Beatles, the German clubs could pay peanuts to English bands hoping that the same might eventually happen to them. We used to do forty-five minutes on and fifteen minutes off. We'd start at eight o'clock and finish about four in the morning. There was an English army camp in Dortmund, and the squaddies would come in and shove a glass of beer towards us on the stage, stuff like that. I didn't drink so I'd pour it away behind a plant pot. They probably thought I could put a lot away, the speed the beer disappeared. The squaddies used to invite us back to their barracks on a Sunday to have a slap-up meal.

Musically it was really good for us. You learn your stuff playing for eight hours every night, not just as musicians, but how to behave on stage, how to keep the attention of the audience and keep them interested. It's not just the music, you have to present it as well, and working long hours, night after night, sharpens you up.

What it also does is show you who's serious and who isn't, and once we got back home, Don and I started wondering about the other guys in the group. We were looking at making a go of things and we talked a lot about what we needed to do, how we could make it happen. We did keep coming back to the fact that quite early on we had tried some recording and John seemed to have struggled with it. Singing in a studio, with headphones on, is different to singing on stage, and John really struggled with that, felt he couldn't quite pitch.

We had done a thing with Bobby Graham, who was the drummer with Joe Brown and the Bruvvers. He was a session musician and had been hired as a producer for Barclay Records, a French label. We did an audition down at Pye Studios. Bobby brought a song along because he used to write with a guitarist called Jimmy Page. 'Little Nightingale' it was called. Jimmy came along with his short hair and his jacket and guitar in a case, and I think he was expecting to play on the track but he didn't because I did it better than Graham was expecting. We were all a bit scared of the studio, but me and Don responded to it. We went in and did our stuff, but John was having problems. We knew we wanted to make records in the future, so from then that was always a worry at the back of our minds.

It wasn't just that, though. The others seemed happy to just drift along and we were probably fracturing a bit musically as well. John and Mick were getting into the mod scene, getting their hair cut like the Who, where me and Don were more interested in the rock scene.

It started getting awkward, and when that happens little things get blown up. Cass bumped his car, which left some paint on a lamp post. One of the others got hold of the paint and Sellotaped it onto his dashboard. Cass pretended not to see it, but one day he went bananas at me. 'I know what they're doing. They've stuck that on there – it's a plot!' Cass was going out with a girl whose father had a greengrocer's business. I think he was starting to feel there was no future in the group, and so one night he just said, 'I'm leaving, I'm going to go and run the grocer's.'

That was the nudge that me and Don needed to form a new band without any of the other three. I must admit we weren't very up front about what we were thinking because we really didn't want to lose the name the 'N Betweens because it was a valuable commodity. It was a good way of getting work, and now we were professional, we needed the work and the money.

The first step was obvious anyway: whatever group we were going to have, we needed a bass player. We put an advert in the local paper, the *Express & Star*, and then held auditions at the Blue Flame in February 1966. We had all kinds of extraordinary people turning up, but there were two people we made a note of. One looked like Mick Jagger but wasn't a very good bassist, but we wondered if we should have him because of his looks and teach him to play better. The other was Jim Lea. Jim was dead young – he looked like a kid coming out of school with his guitar in a plastic bag – but actions speak volumes.

At sixteen, he was three years younger than me and Don, which is a big deal at that age, but he got this McCartney-style violin bass out of his bag and just got up on stage. He didn't play all the root notes like any old bassist, he played it like a guitar. It was like watching Jimi Hendrix grabbing hold of a bass and bending notes. He was really exciting.

Jim was in a band called Nick and the Axemen, and he'd seen us play on a blues/rock night with Georgie Fame, Zoot Money and the Spencer Davis Group, which at the time included Stevie Winwood. The place was packed. He had liked what he heard, and that persuaded him to audition for us, not that he knew what Don and I had got in mind! We were looking further down the road and had our eye on this bloke who was playing guitar and doing a bit of singing with the Memphis Cutouts, Noddy Holder. At the time it wasn't because of Nod's voice, it was more to do with the fact that he came out front and did the odd song and he was good at talking to the audience when he did. We felt he had something about him.

Maybe these things are meant to be, because after finding Jim, Nod kind of fell into our laps. The one day

I bumped into him outside Beatties, the big department store in Wolverhampton, and I persuaded him to come and have a cup of coffee: 'I want to ask you something.' I said we were looking for a singer because Don and I were looking to leave our group and we already had a bass player in mind – not that Jim knew any of that. So Nod said, 'I might be interested – I've just left my group. Can I come and see you playing?' He came and saw us at the Willenhall Baths. There were some things he liked and some things he didn't like, but what he did say was, 'Yes, I'm in.'

I said I'd not seen anyone play a bass like Jim, so, 'Why don't me and you go and have a chat with him?' So off we went in the group's van, pulled up outside Jim's house and there he was at home, playing his violin! I hadn't known that he could read music, all I knew at that stage was that he was a great bass player, really unusual.

I introduced Nod and explained that he was going to be our new singer and that the band we were asking Jim to join wasn't going to have the old singer, nor Mick on guitar anymore. 'There's me, Nod and Don, because the old band are splitting up.' That wasn't what Jim had auditioned for and not what he had seen when he saw us on stage at the Spencer Davis gig. He wasn't sure and we had to be a bit creative to get him on board, to be honest! Jim didn't know anything about Nod, he'd liked the 'N Betweens as we were and he needed to think it through.

Luckily, I'd got the use of the van with the gear in it because we needed to try things out without letting the others know that we were up to something. Nod suggested we rehearse in a place he knew, the Three Men in a Boat on the Beechdale Estate in Walsall, right opposite where he lived. We set our stuff up, and the first song we played was Otis Redding's 'Mr. Pitiful'. We played, and it just took off, there was something happening, it sounded right from the very start.

It wasn't just the sound either, it was the look of the four of us. Probably the Beatles thing was in our minds, but there was something strong about the look of the four of us, like it was really concentrated, nothing spare. From that point we thought, *We are going to do this. This is the group.*

Then it was difficult because obviously we had two new people in the group. Mick left pretty much immediately, but John stayed a bit longer because we had some shows booked. Back then people were in and out of bands all the while so it wasn't that unusual, but it still put a few noses out of joint. I got blamed for breaking the band up, which was a big deal in Bilston. There was quite a bit of hostility, and it always seemed to be me that got the blame for everything, never Don! A girlfriend of John's slapped me across the face the one night, at another gig somebody poured a pint of beer into my bag with all my stage clothes in it, so it was all a bit dicey for a little while.

But in the end it was the only thing for it because me and Don were very serious about making this music business work. On top of that, John was going in a different direction, and in the finish he joined a group called Blues Ensemble with some guys who were regular musicians at the Cedar Club in Birmingham.

Before that though we had a week booked at the 400 Ballroom in Torquay, a residency, and the club insisted that he stay on and do the shows, and that was pretty awkward because all five of us were in a caravan together. John was a bit fed up with it all, and while we were down there we got offered an extra gig in Plymouth, but John had already arranged to go out that night with a girl he'd met in Torquay. So he said, 'Do you fancy doing the gig tonight without me?' Bloody great, of course we didn't! And that was our first gig as a four-piece, miles away from home, giving us a chance to try things out and see how we worked together. Nod knew the songs, so he would take over the singing.

So off we go to this club and I'm looking around and I'm thinking everybody seemed to be cross-eyed. We were playing away and I turned to Nod and said, 'Have you noticed something? They're cross-eyed!' He said, 'Yeah, I know!' When we came off all of us had noticed it individually. That became an in joke – we'd look up at one another and somebody would go cross-eyed.

But it was a great gig. It just worked and it was a fantastic feeling on stage. We were beaming as we packed up and were excited that we'd played together and that we'd really enjoyed it, we could see something there to work on. So back we went to the caravan, full of ourselves, and when we got there, this girl had stood poor John up. He had been alone all night in the caravan and he was really pissed off.

So we get into bed, and I'm sharing with Jim, who is under the sheets, Don and Nod are in another and John is in the third. Jim pulls the blanket and it makes a draught, so John says, 'Make a bloody draught, why don't you, Jim!' He was really fed up about what had happened and we were under the sheets laughing. We were in stitches, but it must have been a real downer for John that he had asked us to do a gig on our own and then got stood up.

By that time the band was really cooking, and I remember John saying, 'It's a pity I'm leaving,' and that was awkward. At the last gig it got a bit emotional, as if he was sorry to be going. 'We sound pretty good, don't we?'

We did, but it was only going to be the four of us from then on.

4

THE BAHAMAS AND BECOMING SLADE

Coming back home from Devon, we just ploughed on as the 'N Betweens, not that everybody was too chuffed about that. Our agency, Astra, weren't keen on us as a four-piece. We didn't seem to be their favourites anymore, put it that way! It was all pubs and hotels that they booked their bands into, so their policy was to have groups that played top-twenty material, and we didn't do that. We wouldn't give in.

We were playing R & B and some obscure American stuff we had got off the Diskery – we spent hours there. That was the music we liked and the music that suited Nod's voice because he most certainly wasn't a blues singer. He could recognise very quickly what would work for him and what wouldn't. He was probably a bit more soulful, soft and a bit nasally in his vocal, not the belter at that stage. We had a song called 'You Better Run', originally a Young Rascals tune, and it sounds a little bit nasal. It's certainly not like the stuff he'd become known for later on.

We were getting more gigs further afield, and in August 1966 we went down to support Crispian St Peters at Tiles on Oxford Street in London. That was a happening place, and while we were playing in walks Kim Fowley, a big record producer, and he loved us: 'You guys know how to project!' He wanted to record us, and within a few days we were in a studio, Regent Sound in Denmark Street, where the Stones had recorded.

We recorded a few things, but 'You Better Run' was set up as the A-side. On the B-side was a new song called 'Evil Witchman'. The single came out on Columbia that December and did really well at home, but Kim's attention span was short, and by then he was off on his next big thing! Still, it was our first number one – in Wolverhampton anyway.

It didn't matter that much to us that Kim disappeared because we all felt that something really strong was happening between the four of us. There was a lot of input from all of us when it came to the songs we covered, how we worked on stage, everything. There was a lot of interest in formulating music, we had a seriousness about us in that sense, we got down to work when we had to. We worked at becoming a really good band because however good the chemistry is, you've still got to work at it.

We could be funny too. We were entertaining – Nod and I were very much into that side of things, especially in pubs because people are not only listening to you but are right up close. We used to play the George Hotel in Walsall on a Sunday night, which was big time then. The

54

stage was dead low and the audience were almost at face level with you, but we had worked on an act, getting on the speaker cabinets – we were always getting on pub chairs to see over the top of crowds.

For the set list, the rule of thumb was that when we'd come across an interesting sound on a record at the Diskery, Jim would take some thoughts away and work on his own ideas, and when he'd written something new we added a quirky style to the way we played the song. I didn't play like other guitarists, there were certain structures to my chords; Don could really make it swing, Jim was a very different bassist, Nod was slowly developing his voice and was a really funny frontman. We played stuff nobody else did and in a way that nobody else did, so we stood out very quickly. It came very naturally. Right from the start, the four of us had quite a heavy sound but without being heavy rock. That meant we were ideal for supporting bands like Cream when they came to town.

We also had a very different sound on stage, a split sound, or stereo, and that was an idea from Swin – Graham Swinnerton, a friend of ours who worked with us and helped out with the gear. Rather than just hearing the bass player on one side of the stage, you could hear everything everywhere. It was really clever and led to people saying we had such a big sound, because if you think about it, if you stand close to the stage you hear the bass player coming off, don't you? Or further over, you hear the rhythm, or the lead. That's what it's like for the punters, and of course even the PA in the early days wasn't miked. We weren't coming out of a PA, only the vocals. The sound on stage was so important, and we were ahead of the game on that one.

We put the hours in – and the miles. I remember in February 1967 we played in Brierley Hill near Dudley on Friday night, we did one show in Kilmarnock and another in Ayr on the Saturday, then we were back playing in Walsall on the Sunday! That was pretty typical of our planning: we'd go anywhere that would have us, whenever they wanted us. I don't know how Betsey, our old Austin J2 van, coped. It's lucky my dad was a mechanic. He kept her running. Just as well really, because we played around 120 gigs that year, building a following and getting better at what we were doing.

We had an opportunity to do some recording that year as well because we were still attached to Columbia/EMI from the Kim Fowley single. We were in Abbey Road Studios in April 1967 – while the Beatles were recording *Sgt. Pepper* as it turned out. We worked with Norman Smith as producer on a song called 'Delighted To See You', but Norman wasn't so delighted with it and nothing came of the session. EMI weren't interested in us.

We kept working away in the clubs. There were a lot of places we played regularly, and we had some good support slots with Cream, John Mayall's Bluesbreakers, the Herd and a few others, but we were starting to get a bit disenchanted with being on the same circuit, playing the same places. Stuck in the van going from one place to another, we were definitely starting to question our management and just where we were going when they suddenly pulled a real rabbit out of the hat.

In May 1968 we got one of the most bizarre bookings of even our career. It turned out a bit like one of those Sixties pop group films, only in real life, but looking back it was a bit of a turning point for the band. Without that summer I don't know if we would ever have been the band and the people that we became.

Our agency, Astra, got an offer for us from a guy called Ken Mallin. He was from Willenhall originally, right on our patch, but now he was living in the Bahamas, on an island called Freeport. Nobody knew how he'd come to be living out there, but anyway he wanted to book us. Apparently he'd seen us in our early days as a four-piece and remembered us when he needed a band. He sent a request to our agent to book us at a club on Freeport called Tropicana.

We couldn't believe it. We're a bunch of working-class lads off council estates and it was a bit exotic going to the other side of Wolverhampton. Now we're being asked to go to the Bahamas! I'd never been on a plane because this was before package holidays came in. You'd usually go to Skegness or Rhyl or Tywyn, there was Butlin's, Pontins, that was it. Planes were for the posh people.

It all seemed a bit surreal. Nowadays, you'd be doing Skype calls, sending emails – all that – to check out whether it was straight or not. But back then a phone call to the Bahamas was a pound a minute, which was a fortune. So we couldn't call him up to find out if it was all OK, but the agency said it was for real. They were dealing with him by telex because this was before even faxes.

We were still dubious about it so we went off and saw this old lady who we thought was his mom, still living in Willenhall. She said it was all above board, so who were we to argue? Even then we didn't really believe any of it until the tickets arrived, and they cost a fortune as well! The offer was a residency there, not earning a lot, but it was the Bahamas so we didn't mind. We sent our equipment over ahead of us, on a cargo flight, so it would be there for when we arrived. We were heading out for a month, like a trial period really, and we had open return tickets.

We got on the plane at Gatwick, flying into Nassau, and I was sat next to Nod. It was just freaky, it really was. We looked at each other and couldn't believe we were on a plane, much less that we'd got a month in the Bahamas. When we got there, we were greeted by these girls in grass skirts and each got handed a drink with a flower in it. We weren't drinkers, only tea and pop, so getting drinks from Interflora was a bit over the top for us.

From Nassau we had to get another plane to Freeport, and there we were met by a bloke called King Sniff. Don't worry, the story gets worse. I don't know what his real name was, we never found out, but they called him King Sniff because he was always sniffing things out, getting his nose in everything. He'd got one of those huge American cars, a Mustang I think, like Steve McQueen in *Bullitt,* so we all piled into that, four wide-eyed kids trying to take in all this stuff from a different planet.

He drove us straight to the club where we were going to play, not to the hotel. In the parking lot there was a wooden shack and inside was a bloke called Eric, who apparently was constantly stoned out of his brain. He was having a kip. He woke up and we made some sort of connection with him, even though he was a bit spaced out. We were a bit naive then, we just thought he was drunk!

King Sniff took us into the club, the Tropicana, palm trees outside the door, all the stuff we'd seen in pictures. We had a look round, and to me it still felt odd. 'You really want us lot to play in the Bahamas? And you've got a bloke sleeping in a shed in the car park?' Anyway, we went inside and there were cockroaches climbing up the wall – steamy, very tropical. It was a typical club, tables set up round a bit of a dance floor, drinks on sticks, all that.

King Sniff says, 'We've got a deal for you to stay at the Sheridan Oceanus Hotel,' which was right on the river. So we headed over there and it was a typically American hotel, air conditioning, the works. So you're outside in this extreme humidity, and you walk in and it's beautiful and cool. Even that was weird because we didn't know what air conditioning was. There's not much call for it in Wolverhampton. Back then most of us didn't even have a fridge.

They were very apologetic: 'You don't have a room each.' We'd never had a room each anyway! They thought they were asking us to slum it, but to us it was like being in Hollywood. To make up for it, we were in adjoining rooms with a connecting door. Two in each room, single bed each, but the beds were massive. I shared with Don, Jim with Nod. There was an ice machine, all sorts, and a bidet. 'Don, have a look, in here! They've got a sink to wash your feet in!' That's what I thought it was, I'd got no idea.

King Sniff told us, 'Don't worry about money. Sign everything to the room, we'll look after the bill.' Great! So we got the menu out for room service and it was fantastic. First off we ordered a coffee, and this waiter turned up with his dicky bow on, came in with a tray, and the coffee's in a metal container, everything just so. Me and Don looked at each other. 'This is a bloody lark, innit? We'll have a bit of this!' And I suppose it gave us a bit of a taste for what it would be like if we were successful, living like a Rolling Stone.

We were set up to do three sets a night, half an hour a time, with other acts on in between There was a fire-eater called Prince Badou, a snake charmer, a belly dancer, cabaret stuff, all that caper! It was like being Hope and Crosby in *The Road to the Bahamas* or something.

So Prince Badou – whose real name was Sid – would come on, and Don had to stay on stage to give the drum roll, then he'd be backing the belly dancer. Nod had to drag a cage on stage for the belly dancer to work in. It was chaos really – we were involved in pretty well everything somewhere along the line, a bit like *This Is Spinal Tap* meets *Phoenix Nights*. But we were only young, it was an adventure.

One night we had this chap called Mr Gold ready to come on stage. He painted himself like Shirley Eaton, the girl in *Goldfinger*. He was on after Prince Badou – Sid – but Sid was going down a storm and he was proper milking it, extending his act, while Mr Gold was waiting to go on. He's painted head to toe in gold, but like in the film, if you are covered in paint, your body can suffocate, so he wants to get on, do his bit, get off and get rid of the paint. So he's at the side of the stage, behind the curtain, desperate to get on. On the stage all you can hear is him shouting, 'Get him off!'

But Prince Badou won't shift. We could see these gold hands gradually sliding down the curtain, as if he was dying, so we start to panic: 'Get him on stage quick before it's too late!' The manager comes running down the front and bundles Prince Badou off, and Mr Gold finally gets on just before he conks out!

Then they'd book these supposedly successful acts, who'd come over from Miami and play for a week. There was a girl group called the Twons, would you believe? They were like the Supremes, and they'd do these dance routines. We had to back them, like the Rhythm Revue or the Ikettes with Ike and Tina.

So they'd be singing and they'd do that American thing you'd see on *Soul Train* or something where they'd go, 'And now we're gonna take it to the bass! Come on, bass!' And Jim would walk up and have to start twisting while he was playing. They'd be dancing round him and shaking their heads, and Jim would start mimicking them. Then it would be, 'On drums, the hardest-working man in show business!' 'Play some guitar, Davey!' Every singer would say, 'I'm gonna play a song that I've got a big hit with over in the States,' and we'd play whatever it was. Then the following week the next act would turn up at the club and say, 'I'm gonna play a song that I've got a big hit with over in the States,' and it would be the same song!

From doing that, we got a bit of that soul/Motown thing in our music and we were starting to put on a show as well as just playing. Without really thinking about it or working on it, we were rounding our act out, becoming something a bit different.

We discovered as time went on that we were on the decidedly bohemian side of the island, definitely not the posh side. Andy Scott, who was later in Sweet, was in a group called Elastic Band, and they were in a better club in the centre of Freeport. We were in the alternative place, out of the way, a bit edgy. We'd get a lot of 'What's yo white ass doin' here?' when we were around the club. We had to be careful where we went, which was weird. That kind of racial segregation, that no-go idea, was new to us.

The club was never full. The idea of getting us in was to fill it up because Andy's club was doing great business, and Ken Mallin wanted to copy that. But that was in the safe part of the island. Even then, a lot of white kids still came. I suppose they wanted a walk on the wild side. There were a lot of Americans living there, so that was a big part of the crowd, there to look at the latest English group to come over. Then there were guys from the armed forces based there. It was a real mix.

We were doing OK. We were playing not much beyond midnight, we had some money, weekly pay, signing everything off at the hotel, it was great. As time went on, we started getting to know people on the island, and they introduced us to smoking pot. I ended up going out with a girl whose parents had a swimming pool, it was good fun. Except one day we got a call from the hotel manager, who wanted to come and talk to us about our bill. So before that we went off to the club to find Ken Mallin to see what was going on. Only he'd scarpered! And there, banging on the door, was a big bruiser of a guy, who's come to kill him because he was owed money. Not just any money. The money he'd advanced Ken to bring us over in the first place. And he was not the only one.

Ken reputedly had his sister living there, and she also had something to do with the finances. We'd already met her, but as it all unravelled, it turned out she wasn't his sister at all, she was actually his mom! They were living in a very nice house together but for some reason nobody could know she was his mom. And the woman back in Willenhall who'd waved us off, she was his grandma.

While all this was going on, there were riots on the island because of the jobs situation. What we hadn't been told was that there was a lot of tension between the locals and foreigners who'd come over and taken their jobs as waiters and in hotels. At one point we watched a guy running past our room carrying a spear, chasing one of the foreigners. It was like watching *Zulu*. We got told to stay inside, it wasn't safe to be on the streets. So we went back to the hotel, and we're sitting there with the debt to pay to the hotel which ran to $2,000, a fortune. Then the club management got fired, and an American came in from somewhere to take charge and he decided to keep us on. He struck a deal with the hotel to pay part of our wages directly to them, but only on the understanding that we stayed on the island until the bill was paid, so our one month there ended up being three. We also got shifted out of our rooms, which were fancy ones, and got stuck in an apartment down the road, where the hotel staff stayed.

The four of us were living in one room with four beds, a fridge and a toilet. That's it. It sounds horrendous, but I think that was what made the band. That's how we got really close. We had to spend that much time cooped up in that room together we came out of it so tight. That set us up for being Slade and going through what came at us after that. It gelled everything. We learned how to live with one another, and years later, when we had all that massive success and were under siege in dressing rooms and cars and hotels all the while, we could handle it because we knew how to cope.

We were also lucky because we'd made friends on the island in that first month, and we'd go round their houses to eat, and there was a roster of them that kept us going. But we couldn't get hold of anybody in England to let them know that we were in trouble. Because we were so far away, it was easy for everybody to ignore us. In fact, the agency was sending telexes to the club to see if they wanted any more groups to join us out there! We were pretty narked by it all. We got left to our own devices and didn't get any help.

But we still had our job at the club, although the new manager was a stronger character and he was laying the law down. Then another character turned up, the Iceman. He was the guy who knew everything, he was into all that was going on. He became a big friend of ours but he was on the payroll at the club. They got him to put this bulb above us on stage, and if it came on, it meant we were too loud and we had to turn it down. The one night the manager's wife turned the bulb on, but we just carried on and ignored it. So she came down the front, pointing at the bulb, shouting at us. We started laughing, and she stormed off to get her husband, who told the Iceman, 'Get a pair of scissors and cut the singer's strings off his guitar.' He got on stage but said to Nod, 'Boss says I've got to cut the strings, man. Just make it look like I'm cutting them!' But we just carried on playing!

It must have been the heat – it was boiling hot all the time we were there – but we did some daft things. I decided to have my hair cut off so that it would grow back thicker. This girl I was going out with suggested I get a Beatle wig, so that sounded OK and I went and got one, fifty dollars. It wasn't a proper one, wasn't pinned down, it shifted about all the time. But it was OK when it was in the right place. I looked pretty cool, like a Beatle, and then I met somebody who wanted to use an English guy to advertise their clothes, flowery shirts and shorts, sneakers. They wanted me to model for them, and seeing as things were rough, I thought it was a way of earning a bit of extra money. The other lads were taking the mick because nobody wore flowery shirts in the Midlands back then. They thought it was hilarious, but I didn't mind any of that.

I put the gear on in the apartment, I've got the wig on, and I walk down to the swimming pool where they're having the fashion show, and there's a guy on the mic: 'Here's Dave wearing our flowery shirt and shorts combination.' That kind of thing. Meanwhile, Jim's writing to his girlfriend Louise saying, 'H has gone off his rocker and started wearing women's clothes!' But I got a bit of money out of it, which was the main thing.

Those were the days when the kaftan thing was popular, and I fancied one. So a couple of days later I was in a shop and I saw this long denim dress which fastened up the front with buttons, and I thought that it might look a bit like a kaftan, so I bought it and put it on. Unfortunately, it only came down to my knees, but I thought I could get away with it.

We went to the club to do the show that night – I'm still wearing my dress – and this tall, blonde girl walked in with an American guy and she was wearing exactly the same dress. I was on stage, playing away, and she came down the front and screamed, 'He's got my dress on! He's a weirdo!' So the rest of the band were just taking the piss out of me and I became the focal point of things all of a sudden. That was the first time that I really looked different on stage and that was the start of that side of the band.

By then we were starting to get a bit fed up of it all and were wondering how to get home. We heard the club wanted to redecorate to encourage more trade and they told us to have a week off while they were closed. So we thought, *Great. This is our chance!* We took all the equipment out, went to the airport, and used our open return tickets to send the gear home by cargo plane. Then we booked a flight out of Freeport to Nassau and were getting ready to go.

Meanwhile, I owed this girl fifty dollars for the Beatle wig, and she'd got wind of the fact I was doing a runner. Her brother was built like Superman, huge, so Nod was winding me up: 'He's gonna come looking for you, H!' So I hopped on a flight to Nassau a day early, ahead of the other lads, just to get away. I got there late at night and then had to wait for them to arrive the following day.

I was starving and so decided to walk into Nassau, which was about twenty minutes away, to get something to eat, because everything in the airport was closed. It was pitch black and I was walking down this road, past these shacks – and I mean real shacks, proper run-down. I came to what looked like a village, and after what we'd seen in Freeport, I was pretty uncomfortable. I was trying to find my way round the edge of it all, but these black guys had clocked me so I decided to turn back.

Then I had the bright idea to go and sleep on the beach because I'd read James Bond books where he'd done that. So I went and lay down on the sand and started nodding off, but then I heard this hissing. I looked up, and it was a huge crab with its claws out, rearing up, coming towards me. I'm knackered and this giant bloody crab is coming to kill me!

I got up and ran off and down the road until I came across a few houses. The lights were off, no idea if there was anyone about, so I looked for an open window, just to get in and get some sleep. I managed to get in a garage. I lay down again, and then I heard something. The place was full of cockroaches and they were climbing up the walls. So I ran out of there and headed back to the airport. When I got there, I just got in somebody's car – nobody locked stuff – and fell asleep.

The day after, the rest of the band arrived, and they'd got away no problems at all. When I saw them getting off the plane, I'd never been so happy to see the three of them – Nod, Jimmy and Don plus my Burns guitar, which I'd left with Don for safekeeping. He was carrying it in a polythene bag.

Even then, we were still on edge because we knew we weren't away yet. We didn't know if they'd send anybody after us, and in the airport we kept out of the way. Then our flight got delayed and we were really paranoid by now. Everybody looked like a gangster, there were all these people in shades, so we thought they were looking for us – but it was the Bahamas, everybody wore shades! It felt like we'd escaped from Colditz. Eventually we boarded the plane, and when it took off, it really did feel as if we'd escaped back to Blighty.

We were now a completely different band – the trip had had a really profound effect on us. The way we sounded, how we looked, the people we were, everything was different. We played our first gig back home in Bilston; loads of friends came to see us, and they all said we sounded different. We weren't as full on, we were a bit quieter, you could hear the music more. I had short hair, I got rid of the wig, we were all suntanned. We came back with different songs, 'Journey To The Centre Of Your Mind', 'Born To Be Wild', things that ended up on the *Beginnings* album.

It was a very influential period for us. We took on a lot of different ideas about everything, not just the music, but the way we dressed, how we behaved. You look at the cover of *Beginnings* a bit later and it has an American feel to it. We were doing covers of Steppenwolf, Zappa, Marvin Gaye, but we were still four blokes from the Black Country, that was definitely in there as well, but we'd lived a bit now, we'd seen a few things.

We might not have changed our name yet, but there's no doubt about it. Now we were Slade.

5

BEGINNINGS

When we got back from the Bahamas, we hadn't just changed musically, we'd become tougher as people and even more determined to make things happen in our career. We were so tight as a unit now after all we'd gone through and decided we'd had enough of being managed and represented by Astra. We were stuck on the same circuit in the Midlands and the North pretty much, and we knew that if we were going to get anywhere, we needed to spread out and especially get people in London to take notice of us. Not only that. We'd been left to our own devices out in the Bahamas – there'd been no help for us when things went wrong – and that left a bad taste in the mouth. We were really narked with Astra, so we were determined that we were going to start making things happen.

A bloke called Andy the Copper appeared at this point, who had an agency with his wife Anita Anderson, though as a policeman he kept it quiet. But he was interested in us and ran a gig called the Ship and Rainbow, a room at the back of the Hollybush in

Wolverhampton. That was one of the first shows we played after we got back from the Bahamas, and it was an important venue because it not only had pop music but also our type of music. It had a Thursday blues night and a Saturday pop night, and used to have all sorts of weird and wonderful things. So we signed up with him and the Anita Anderson Agency.

Things picked up pretty fast then. Roger Allen was a partner in the agency and he had a friend called Irving Martin, who was close to Jack Baverstock, who was the A & R boss at Fontana. We didn't realise at the time, being a bit naive, but that was how the music business worked: making contacts and knowing the right people. We got called down to do a recording audition in London on 3 December 1968 and did two tracks with Irving, 'Journey To The Centre Of Your Mind' and 'Blues In E'. He passed them on to his boss, and Jack liked what he was listening to, so much so that we were back on the 11th to record four more.

I remember he called me into his office after that and said, 'I think you're good, but you'll never get anywhere up north, you need London connections.' And he was right: in those days you definitely did. What it boiled down to was that he was willing to give us a record deal, but only if we got some management in London. He said he knew people and was prepared to give them a call. We didn't even consult the agency back home, we just told him to get on with it. What came out of that was we got involved with a bloke called John Gunnell. John and Rick Gunnell were known quite well around the clubs in

London at the time. They were involved with the Robert Stigwood Organisation, so they were real players on the scene.

The other thing was that Jack hated the name of the group and insisted we changed from the 'N Betweens. Initially someone came up with Nicky Nacky Noo, which hung around for a couple of weeks before we saw some sense and dropped that, and then we became Ambrose Slade. Jack offered a money prize to anyone on the Fontana staff who could up with a name, and this woman there had a name for everything she owned. She had a purse called Ambrose and a mirror called Slade, and there we were, Ambrose Slade!

It still wasn't great, but Jack liked it and he was going to put us in the studio and make a record at last, so we put up with it and took on the new name from the start of 1969. Fontana were so happy with us, we were named their 'most promising' band of the year, and got sent out to represent them at a festival in Holland in January.

Things had moved pretty quick that December, because we had also done some filming at Euston Station in London, going up and down the escalators, running around the main waiting area, your typical sort of Sixties promo film, which was going to be used for our first single – not that anybody knew what that was going to be yet. What's funny is that the other three were in dark suits, and there's me in a white jacket and bright orange flares, standing out already!

Jack offered us some more free studio time, the first two days in January 1969 when probably nobody else wanted to record anyway, and we basically put down our live show on tape with a few silly songs and the odd stupid track. It was fun, but it probably wasn't focused enough, and that was probably because I felt we'd never had strong management but had been left to our own devices. Sometimes you need somebody else to tell you what's working and what isn't.

One of the things Jack did suggest was that we write some of our own material, which was sensible given the way the business was moving, with most bands recording their own songs after the Beatles and the Stones had gone in that direction. It was a bit late in the day for our first album, and we ended up with only four out of twelve songs on there, three of them written by the four of us and 'Pity The Mother' by just Nod and Jim, who of course ended up being Slade's songwriting team.

Looking back at that first record, it was a very different Slade to what we became because, as I say, we'd never been given any real direction, and though we worked with a guy called Roger Wake in the studio, we were effectively producing ourselves. At that point we were still very influenced by what we'd picked up in the Bahamas, so although as people we were still a pretty earthy bunch of Black Country boys, musically we were fixated on a lot of the stuff we had heard over there. This had the bonus that not many people over here knew about it. So we'd heard this Frank Zappa record before most people in Britain knew who he was, and liked 'Ain't Got No Heart', it really inspired us with some new ideas, and that was something quite new.

We were finding our way. These were times when everything was changing. It was *Sgt. Pepper*, the underground, psychedelia, flower power in 1967, then coming out of that into the violence of '68. Things were moving so fast. Add the exposure we had to American music into that and then the fact that it was our first real chance to record anything more than a single, it's no wonder *Beginnings* was a bit varied.

The scene was still very much split between the pop end of things and the more underground side. When we played 'Journey To The Centre Of Your Mind' in a place where they had drinking people wanting to hear what was in their local charts, we wouldn't get another gig there, but we were sticklers for not changing because we wanted to be ourselves. Other groups would work in pubs, Sunday lunchtimes, Mecca ballrooms because they wanted pop bands and pop music. But there was the other side of it, the hip clubs. There was a place in Erdington near Birmingham, Mothers, and if you got a gig there, they all wore leather clothes and danced a bit funny. If you got in there, they weren't playing pop music, that's for sure.

Beginnings was more or less our live set list, as the first album is for a lot of groups. Because of that, it did cover a few different musical areas because even a band like us, when you're playing live, you do try and get everybody interested in you, you throw a bone to a crowd that might never have heard of you before by playing something they know.

We weren't completely obscure – we had some songs like 'Martha My Dear' by the Beatles – but a lot of the material was quite different. 'Born To Be Wild', I think people knew by then, and that showed our rock side, then we did a Marvin Gaye number; then you've got 'Journey To The Centre Of Your Mind' by Ted Nugent, which speaks for itself. That was picked up when we were all together in the Bahamas and we learned some odd underground things.

We were experimenting with every aspect of the band at this time. We got into burning incense on the side of the stage – the one show we had to evacuate the club because there was no ventilation and the smoke off the incense was suffocating everybody! This was around the time when the Syd Barrett version of Pink Floyd were in the charts, and they were experimenting with lights, oil on slides. It was a really fun time actually. We weren't quite flowers-in-our-hair types, but we weren't far off.

We did a few of our own songs. We wrote in different combinations, all four of us, individually, pairings, just trying to see what worked. 'Roach Daddy' is to do with drugs after we'd been introduced to marijuana on the Bahamas – everybody had to have a drugs song then. 'Genesis' was the culmination of a riff I played, formulating this instrumental which actually became another song later on, using the same idea.

Probably the biggest difference from the later Slade sound was Nod's voice, because he did struggle a bit at times. I don't think he'd found his niche, his real voice at that point. He was still a bit nasal, probably a bit nervous as well, and I think he preferred to play his voice down and just have it sitting in the mix rather than belting out over the top.

For me it was exciting to be a proper recording band at last. We'd made that promo film and then we went off to shoot the cover for the album sleeve. We did it with a local photographer on top of Pouk Hill, which is near to where Nod lived on that estate in Walsall. I think they've built a housing estate on it now, but it was two ticks from Nod's house. We took our tops off and were mucking around on the rocks. It was freezing, but at least we got a song out of it on the next album, so I suppose that's some consolation.

We finished off the album in February 1969, ready for release, and within the business, people started hearing it straight away. John Gunnell was obviously very well connected, that's why we'd signed up with him, and one of his mates was Chas Chandler. Chas had been the bass player in the Animals, who'd had some big hits like 'House of the Rising Sun'. When that finished, he went into record production and management, and it was Chas who brought Jimi Hendrix over from America and put together the Experience for him. Chas was a big figure – physically as well as in the business!

He got to hear the album and there was something there that he liked, but I don't think he was completely sure about us. He needed to see us play live. We were playing in John Gunnell's club in the West End, Rasputin's, near where Chas had his office. Chas was a bit late getting there, and this club was in the basement of a bigger place. He came down the stairs and thought he was listening to a record, he didn't realise it was us playing live, so we got him straight away. We knew he was coming, and when he arrived, you noticed him because he was a big bloke and that night he'd got his wife Lotta with him, and she was pregnant. They went and sat in the corner, and after we'd finished, it was like something out of a film. He came over to us, like it was in slow motion, and straight away said, 'I want to sign you.' That was it, no introductions, just that. He obviously saw something in us that nobody else had to that point.

He said he saw us as 'a breath of fresh air', that's how he put it. And no doubt he saw a new project. Hendrix was gone, so who else was there? He hadn't found anyone, then he saw us and he was lifted by us. He got off on the way we were, because we were different. In the late 1960s everybody played with their heads down, there was no real contact with the audience, the crowd sat cross-legged on the floor, it was hippies getting stoned, but we were cocky, we put on a bit of a show.

We had a theatrical element to us, and Chas was well up for that, as he would be having worked with Hendrix. Jimi wore some great clothes, the military stuff that he got from Carnaby Street, and he was very theatrical too, setting fire to guitars! Chas saw the potential in that and recognised a different element of that in us. He liked the showmanship side of things.

I remember one of the first things Chas said to me: 'I can just imagine you having this big guitar made. So that you, being little, can have this huge great guitar,' and I'm thinking, *This bloke speaks my language.* He was thinking of something really bizarre. I remember him saying to me – because I'm short – 'We need to think of things that will get you known or seen.'

That side of us was what he reacted to, us as a band and an act that could entertain people, because I don't think he was happy with *Beginnings* at all. That alone wouldn't have got him on our side. No question, he would have discarded that first album if he could. He would have bought the rights and not released it, but he was stuck with it, and he had other fights to win first.

If he was going to manage us, he had to get us out of our existing contract with Anita Anderson, so he invited her down with Andy the Copper. Andy said, 'Don't worry, guys. I won't let you go, I'll look after you,' and then he flogged us for £500 to Chas! It wasn't just the money side of it, I think they recognised that they couldn't compete with Chas. He was big league, a proper operator. Nobody of his stature had come into our lives before. Previous managers were just agents really, putting us in clubs up and down the country, Meccas and the like. Nobody we'd come into contact with was on Chas's level except maybe that brief affair we'd had with Kim Fowley.

Chas had been in a band himself, then he had managed a phenomenal guitarist, so he was a force to be reckoned with. People would listen to him, even though the Hendrix thing was out of the window at that point. He was a sharp businessman, just what we needed at that stage, although I didn't realise quite how businesslike he was, because he later told Swin, who he brought into the team to work on the road with us, 'I just see this as a four-year thing.' We didn't know that. But we did know that Chas loved us, and for the moment that was enough.

6

FROM HIPPIES
TO SKINHEADS

Nearly fifty years on from the release of *Beginnings*, listening to it again, it's hard to associate the group on that record with the group we were on stage. That's not uncommon for bands the first time they go in the studio because it's a new environment, but it didn't really capture who we were when we played live.

It was missing our essence, the energy and power that we were able to generate in a live show. It took Chas to capture and reproduce that in the studio a little bit later. And we were a covers band at that point as well, so whatever we did to the arrangements and the playing of the songs, it still wasn't the real undiluted essence of Slade. That came later on, but at that time the 'Lennon and McCartney of the Black Country', Nod and Jim, hadn't yet uncovered their ability as writers, especially as a partnership.

Saying all of that, even though *Beginnings* failed to chart in 1969, it was a milestone in the band's history as it showcased our talent and potential as a band and gave some clues as to our musical tastes and influences, some of which would resurface on our bestselling *Alive* LP a couple of years later. It was an important record because it gave us a first proper chance at working in a studio and learning about that, ready for next time. We'd cracked it on stage, people were coming to the gigs and loved the whole performance element of the group, but now we were getting the hang of translating that onto tape. And given we knew Chas had heard *Beginnings* before he signed us, I think that gave us confidence and meant we could shrug off the fact that it didn't shift many copies. Right from the off, Chas could see the potential in us and he had a vision of where we could go.

Although the four of us had been together for three years by then and we were a really tight live act, Ambrose Slade was still quite a way from what we were going to become and be recognised for. Like a lot of groups, we started off doing covers of other people's songs and then slowly started piecing together a few of our own. It was still early days for that and on *Beginnings*, there were four songs that we'd written. We were still searching around to find what worked as far as songwriting went, all finding our feet. I wrote a couple of things with Nod, 'Gospel According to Rasputin' and 'Do You Want Me', but we were trying various combinations to see what took off.

Chas was very much behind us writing songs, something that managers were into at the time – Andrew Loog Oldham had locked Jagger and Richards in a room so that the Stones would have original material – and was a clever man. He'd learned a lot from both sides of the industry. He wanted to be involved in everything: the production and the publishing, the way we looked, our image, how we were promoted, everything. He was a great manager, musician and showman. I think he'd seen what people like Mickie Most and Peter Grant were doing in that area. He was ambitious, but so were we, so it was a perfect match in that sense, but the most important thing was that he could recognise a good song. Even if it wasn't finished, he knew what to do with it and how to make it sound like the group that people were used to hearing at the gigs. He could bottle that excitement and then put it on tape.

He was up front about what he wanted as well. He advised us to take on our own solicitor to look over the management deal he offered us. I'm sure we did, but there was no chance we wouldn't want to go with Chas because this was a serious opportunity, he was a big fish.

We'd been a good band for a long time and were happy with the gigs we were doing. Looking back, I would say it was an extremely happy time and in some ways happier than later, despite all the success and fame. Although I loved being successful, I think the joy of what it was like in the early days came from how simple it was, and just how good it felt not to be at Tarmac, not having anybody tell me what to do. There was certainly more freedom then than when we had the hits.

They were simple times of learning songs, going down to St Giles' Youth Centre to rehearse a track after Nod had got the record from the Diskery in Birmingham, pie and chips up at the local caff afterwards, then playing it live that night. There was something really great about all that. Very much like the early Beatles, we slept in vans and on floors, ate in motorway diners in the middle of the night, did all these things together. We still had our own opinions, still went out with our girlfriends, but the band was everything. No matter what was going on, around comes the van, we've got a gig in Scotland for three days or we're up at the Ship and Rainbow, or at the Woolpack restaurant or the Walsall George, Sunday night at the Connaught Hotel, Civic Hall on a Monday night, half a crown in! That was everything to us, life revolved round it.

But we also knew we couldn't do that circuit for ever and we wanted to play the rest of the country, have hits, and Chas was very much the man we thought could make it happen for us. Vice versa as well though, because Chas always said that if he hadn't found us, somebody else would have. He always thought we would be big.

Working the clubs, playing every night, we knew how songs worked, what got people going. Verse, chorus, middle eight. A lot of pop records are two and a half, three minutes long, and they say enough. They're an art form. There's a magic to them because they're real, there's an honesty to them. It was people singing and playing, not just a bloke on a laptop pulling a few sounds in made by someone else or ripping this or that off. Groups like us had to play their instruments and formulate the characteristics that made up the tracks. They're human, they're warm, and that's what people respond to.

It's the chemistry of individuals working together, and you cannot do that with a loop track or a programmed drummer. That's going to be static. Our records weren't cut and pasted; records were done live every time. You'd do the first chorus, then you'd move to the second, but there would be a change in it because you can't do it the same twice. Although you're singing the same words there are characteristics of the moment.

Nod would probably do several takes of his vocal, and they might pull a bit from this one or that one, but they were never identical. But sometimes his initial live performance, the guide vocal, when we were first putting down the track, was used because he's that type of singer. You don't overwork Nod's voice because it doesn't benefit from it. Chas was brilliant in seeing that. Chas used simple ADT echo on his voice, and Nod's voice was big anyhow. It had that sound, though the real power that cut through came a little bit later because Nod wasn't so much a growler early on. I suppose Chas was influenced by working with Eric Burdon in the Animals and saw the potential in Nod to do something on those lines.

We had a strong idea of what we wanted to do but we were still young, still a bit naive, and so Chas was great in directing things at that point. One of the things he wanted to do, like Jack had, was change our name. He thought Ambrose Slade was misleading, as though that was the singer's name – Jethro Tull always had that problem. Ambrose Slade was a bit awkward, and he wanted something a bit more punchy. So by the end of 1969 we were just Slade.

That wasn't the only change he suggested. A lot of managers have a view on how the group is going to look – Brian Epstein putting the Beatles in suits is the classic example of that. In the group I was very much the one interested in fashion, like that early video showed, and I think the others probably disapproved of my flamboyance a bit. The one time we went to a clothes shop in Birmingham – we hadn't been together long – to choose something to wear on stage, our personalities came right out! Jim chose something really dark, I went for something bright yellow, and Nod chose a check jacket.

By the time the first record came out we all had long hair, and we did a photo session with Gered Mankowitz. It was all beads and a bit hippy, and I've got this strange sleeveless top on. We looked good actually, but maybe much like a lot of groups did at the time. Now Chas started talking about us changing our image ahead of making the next album. He was after something that would make us stand out.

Then Keith Altham started with us as a publicist. He'd worked with the Stones and the Beatles, and he was the one who suggested to Chas that we go skinhead, which wasn't something that I'd ever have thought of. To be honest, I hated it, but Chas was very convincing, so we gave in. I think he felt it was a chance to cash in on the skinhead thing, which was popular across the country, so we went to the barbers and had our hair cropped. We looked like a bunch of hooligans. When I went home my dad said, 'Looks all right that!'

Our next gig was on the Isle of Arran in Scotland. Skinheads like reggae music and ska, and we definitely weren't a reggae band; we were playing rock and we'd got a violin player in the group! We hid in the dressing room because the audience was a bit rough, and when we got on stage, there were all these skinheads with jeans and braces. It was bizarre. We stayed in the dressing room for ages afterwards for fear of them beating us up because we weren't genuine.

We wanted to put out a single now we had a new image, but we were looking for a song. We ended up recording 'Wild Winds Are Blowing', a song by Jack Winsley and Bob Saker, which came out on Fontana under the name The Slade. It was quite an aggressive record, but it didn't do anything in the charts at all.

Being a skinhead was bloody uncomfortable too, I do remember that. We were all looking pretty good up to that point, and then we did that. Terrible! I had been going out with a blonde girl at the time, Jane, and I remember her father was something big at Alton Towers. She was really posh. It was when the Love Affair were in the charts because that is how I met her. We did a show, and the Love Affair were on too, and she was sitting in a bar, and I was fascinated by posh girls. She had a car as well – I didn't – so she was even more fascinating!

When we met I had the George Harrison look with long hair. I went out with her for a while, but the one day I rang her up and said that our manager wanted us to have our hair cut. I remember saying to her, 'He says if I do this, I'll be a millionaire.' I was a sucker for that! There's me living with my mom and dad in a council house as a potential millionaire. But on this occasion Chas was very persuasive. He was great at sowing a seed in your mind. Anyway, this girl wasn't as gullible as me because that was the last I saw of her. The posh girl wasn't going to be seen dead with a skinhead!

That turned out for the best actually because just after that, as we were coming out of the skinhead period, we were playing at the Connaught in Wolverhampton and I met a girl called Jan...

7

JAN

I think a lot of people think blokes join bands, particularly in the 1960s, so that they could 'pull birds', but if you are going to make a band work and be successful, it's got to be about the music and about the band's chemistry first and foremost. If you haven't got that, then you won't be around for five minutes. The public aren't daft. And then if you're successful, especially on the scale that we were, you don't have time for anything but the band! I wasn't without experience, put it like that, but like I say, for all of us it was band first, girlfriends second, and the girls had to put up with that. The funny thing is that when I did 'pull' the woman I was going to marry, Jan, she wasn't that bothered about music or even interested in me being in a band. That may be one of the reasons why we're still together nearly five decades later.

At school I wasn't very confident. I have always had a prominent mouth and I broke my front tooth because a kid chucked me over his shoulder. Mom was annoyed: 'You've spoilt your mouth!' There was no dental capping going on then, so I was self-conscious about that as well as my ears. But coming out of school around 1961, I had a long-standing girlfriend called Pat Leighton who was a really nice girl. She was with me quite some time, to the point when the Beatles made it and the fringes were going on. Pat was the first person who combed my hair forward and tried to cut my fringe like George Harrison, and I remember she did it in the front room of our house. She cut my fringe and then we went out and I thought, *This is pretty good actually*. But Mom disapproved, and I was still working at Tarmac, so I had to comb my hair back again. It was a flip-flop between pushing my hair forward when I went out with the band, and combing it back when I came home.

When the band started playing further afield, I finished with Pat because I didn't want to be tied down. That led to a girl in Torquay. Before he was with us, Nod had been in a band called Steve Brett and the Mavericks and their drummer went out with a girl who lived in a hotel in Torquay, run by her mom and dad. This is August 1965 – I know that because the Walker Brothers were number one with 'Make It Easy On Yourself'. I couldn't go out with her because of this drummer, but then I got a message that they'd split up and the two of us just clicked.

She came up to the Midlands to meet my mom and dad and all the rest of it, and before long she moved in with us and became a big friend to my sister. With her mom and dad having the hotel, it seemed quite exciting, and I did have quite a long-standing relationship with her. Then we went to the Bahamas and I was terrible at writing letters, and her mom and dad came up and took her home because they felt like I had buzzed off – which I had really. I was very random in those days. I had been thinking about getting married or engaged, but she went back to Torquay and that was that.

After that I met Jane from Alton Towers, but there were always arguments. Basically it wasn't working and my skinhead haircut was the final straw! I was also going out on and off with a girl called Angela who was a friend of Carol, but that didn't work out either. She ended up being Don's girlfriend, with tragic consequences a few years later.

So I hadn't got a girlfriend this night we played the Connaught in Wolverhampton, a regular Sunday gig. Jan had finished with her boyfriend and she'd got nothing to do on this Sunday night, and her dad said to Ron, her brother, 'Why don't you take your sister to the Connaught?' Jan was actually best friends with Nod's girlfriend Pam, so that was one reason why she came.

So Ron brought her in and I clocked her. I'll always remember she was in a white dress with holes in it, like crêpe. She was blonde and you wouldn't miss her, not how she looked. Pam introduced me to her: 'This is my friend Jan.' I was chatting to her and said I would give her a lift home, so Ron scooted off and left her with me because Pam was there. Jan was a bit suspicious, of course, probably on account of the cropped hair. But I took her home and I just said, 'Do you fancy going out somewhere?' as you do. There was a local DJ called Barmy Barry, he was very well known in the sixties. He used to have discos in pubs. I knew where he was playing and so I said, 'Do you fancy going?' And from there we started going out.

I remember going round to see her mom and dad the first time. She had a little sister, Julie, and I took her a present, a knitted fish. No idea why! I bought her mom something daft as well, though I can't remember what. Probably just as well! Her mom and dad were pretty sceptical, I was just this no-hoper in a pop group, which around 1969, 1970 was about as low as you could go for parents.

I don't think they liked me; I think they thought I was leading Jan astray. Julie always remembers when Jan was getting ready to go out with me, her dad saying, 'You ain't going out in that!' It was the miniskirt time, and Jan very definitely had the figure for it. Julie would be there, grabbing the bottom of her skirt, pulling it a bit lower! I'd got a Sunbeam Alpine and I suppose I was a bit flash, so her mom and dad were very suspicious of me at first. They were thinking, *He hasn't got any future* – Jan told me that. I know they'd also quite liked previous boyfriends too. And the car had reclining seats as well, which Jan didn't like. But I'd got my guitar behind the passenger seat, so she thought she'd be safe.

Then we were dumping the skinhead thing and I was growing my hair again, but it wasn't developing into anything normal because the skinhead look then evolved into the funny haircuts we got famous for. I have never had thick hair and so I just grew a short fringe and had it long at the sides. Nod didn't grow the top at first, he just grew the sideboards. As my hair grew, so I started getting into the long boots and all that.

Jan saw me as unusual and a little bit weird, but she liked this and the strange clothes, and then I started to buy her clothes. I was very into fashion. The one time I took her to London for a gig and brought her back through the night, and it was snowing so it took ages to get home. I was dropping Jan off, and her mom was getting ready for work as Jan was coming in, looking all white-faced with the tiredness, not having slept. That didn't go down well, but it was a fantastic time in our lives, post-1960s, hippies, colours – great days they were. I took Jan to Kensington Market one time, and Jan is one of those girls who you put clothes on her and it happens, she looks amazing. There were these long coats with moons on, a bit wizardy. I dressed her in these bizarre baggy flares and all that kind of thing, she looked fabulous.

Couple of days later she was standing at the bus stop, and one of the neighbours who didn't know her but knew Jan's mom, goes past. This neighbour worked with her mom and they were talking and she said, 'I saw something the other day. I've never seen anything like it. There was this girl with a big hippy hat,' and she described the coat and this really bizarre, colourful person. And Jan's mom said, 'That's my daughter.'

It was such a great time. I always remember Chas when I brought Jan down to London. There was all sorts of stuff going on with see-through tops and all that, and Jan wasn't someone you could ignore – anybody from that time would tell you that – and let's face it, I'm a show-off, so I wanted everyone to see this girl who looked so great. I'm like that, I admit it. So I introduced her to Chas and he said, 'Davey, I didn't think girls looked as good as that up north!'

I've had some good fortune in my life, but never more than in meeting Jan, as this book will show. I had it summed up for me not long ago when we met Arthur Brown from The Crazy World Of... We were only talking for a few minutes and he said about Jan, 'Ah! The rock!' That sums it up.

8

PLAYING IT LOUD

Although we were starting to move away from the skinhead look, our second album, *Play It Loud*, featured us still with short hair on the cover – and looking a bit uncomfortable with it – when it came out in November 1970. We were also still wearing the skinhead gear, and Nod and Don especially looked a bit intimidating. Somebody said it looked like we'd just come home from work and were getting ready to go out for a fight!

That wasn't us at all. We were basically peace-loving people, but I think Chas wanted us to play up to the image a bit. He tried to get us chucked out of a posh hotel in London. He booked us in, then we were all in one room and we were making a row. We shoved some chairs in the lift, we were banging on the floor. He wanted SKINHEAD GROUP GET AXED FROM HOTEL in the papers, but they didn't throw us out. Eventually, politely, they asked us to leave, so no story!

It's funny how a haircut changes the way people look at you. Nod looked really hard, Don looked like a Brillo pad, me and Jim really didn't suit it. I remember Chas taking Nod and Jim to an Army and Navy store to get us some clothes. It was totally alien to someone like me, who was used to being flamboyant now, having to wear jeans. We kept it going for a while, but thankfully that look lasted less than twelve months. There was an incident where the producer of *Top of the Pops* had his son beaten up by a skinhead, so from then that look wasn't doing us any favours. Slowly the hair started to grow and Chas said nothing!

Did it work? It did separate us from all the bands that had long hair. They all tended to look like each other so you couldn't tell one from another, whereas folk would remember us. Nod kept the short top and grew the sides and kept the braces, so you might say something came of it. That seemed to suit him though. He had a flat cap and those sideboards, which were great, and he grew his hair eventually.

Some people have said over the years that Nod's voice suited that skinhead look. Jan's dad said that his voice was 'a working man, crying out to be heard', and I think that was eventually a lot of our appeal. We were very much perceived as working blokes who'd come through it all, not manufactured in any way.

Nod's got a lot of passion in his voice, he sang it straight where somebody like Ian Gillan of Deep Purple was doing that screaming, high vocal. Nod didn't do that, his was grittier, a growl. I think people could identify with it, but even on *Play It Loud*, it was all still coming together, we were still finding our niche a bit. We had intricate, interesting harmonies, yet we never sang light, we were quite loud. Saying that, the reason *Play It Loud* is called that is because we never thought the band sounded loud enough on the actual album. It still wasn't quite there.

That was the first time we went in the studio with Chas, and he was very influential. He might let you set up your stuff, but then he'd say you needed this or that and you had to listen to him. Chas was quite a fatherly figure, someone who was quite encouraging with me. Very early on he told me that my face was my fortune, and I'd never heard anyone say that! He was also very positive about my ability as a guitarist. He saw the originality and said a lot of kind things about me to other people, which I would find out later. I know he loved the sound of the band, Nod's voice and Jim's bass playing and Don's drumming. There were things about us all, but the whole picture is what he saw and what he fell in love with. He had a great ear. When Chas was on the case, he was on the case.

When we were recording Chas wouldn't use the big gear from stage. He said he'd had problems with Hendrix wanting to use the stack too loud and that just didn't work on tape: 'It will be distorted and it just won't be big.' So his advice was always to use a small amp. We'd rehearse, take the group's gear to his barn, and he would help pick the songs.

We didn't have a great understanding of recording, we were pretty green at that point. The studio is a bit of a nervy environment for a lot of artists who think they sound great live because it's a different ball game. You're suddenly vulnerable, you don't sound quite how you thought you did, so we did go through a learning process. We would just get the drums down really and then we would replace everything else. Jim was quite a busy bass player – like a lead player, he used to play fast – and Chas had an influence on how he recorded, being a bass player himself. You'd get a basic take with the right feel and the right tempo, and all those hit records were worked the same, Nod singing live, and you would sometimes keep that vocal. Nod is not the sort of vocalist where you can keep doing takes. He actually loses it, so we'd often use the guide vocal.

The big thing on *Play It Loud* was we only had three cover versions out of the twelve songs, and that was a proper step forward for us, although it was still a bit tentative. There were nine originals. 'Know Who You Are' was a rewrite of 'Genesis' from the first album: we turned it from an instrumental into a song. That was my only writing credit, where Jim had a hand in all nine. Funnily enough, so did Don. They were doing a lot of the writing at that point, and Nod helped out on five of the tracks. We still hadn't found that writing team of Jim and Nod yet.

Successful bands are always more than the sum of the parts. Something special happens when the right group of individuals come together, and what they create as that unit becomes the band. That was definitely true about us because we all had different strengths, different things that we brought to the party. My strength, especially in those early years, was bringing that element of showmanship to things with the way I looked, the way I played. I was possibly more of the driving force for us on stage. Ultimately, Jim and Nod would take that role in the songwriting department, and Don's unique drumming style gave us something else that helped get people's ear.

We were a real band, four people contributing, and I loved that about us because it is something special when a group of people all work for the common good. We were recognising and developing those strengths, learning what worked and what didn't, creating the Slade that people would come to know and love. It was a massive effort from all of us – and Chas – to create that.

My attitude to it at the time was, 'You write 'em, I'll sell 'em!' That's a bit tongue-in-cheek, but there's a lot of truth in there. The sound I had, the way I behaved, the way-out clothes I wore, they were a big part of what Slade was, and I poured all my energies into that and didn't really dabble much in songwriting at that stage. Later on I did get frustrated when I brought songs to the band and they got turned down, so I was in the George Harrison role again then as well!

The covers were a real mix. 'Shape Of Things To Come' was from a film and the lead-off single to the album; we did a version of 'Could I', which had been recorded by Bread, and there was a Neil Innes song, 'Angelina'. But this was a time when there was still every kind of music in the charts. You had the Who, the Stones; the Beatles were just finishing, but the four of them had solo singles; then you had American things, there was the cheesy stuff, bubblegum pop, comedy records, crooners – it was a real mixture.

Even in the late 1960s a lot of big bands were still around too, so when we did the Civic or the Beatties staff dance there was Ted Heath, Kenny Ball with his *Midnight in Moscow*, and they were really good. They'd be top of the bill. You'd got guitar players and amps and then you'd got that.

It was the same when we recorded, especially when we went to do something for the BBC when we were trying to get on *Sounds of the Seventies*. It was two-track recording, so it was playing live. We were in Maida Vale, and there was this engineer smoking a pipe, wearing a white coat. Our amplifier had a booster, but the booster made a rumbling sound until we started playing, and then in went the guitar and that rumble disappeared. When he heard it he pulled a face: 'Urgh, leakage. It sounds like porridge.' We were cracking up. Even the Beatles' *A Hard Day's Night* from a few years before reflects that tension between the generations, that being told what to do. 'I fought the war for people like you!' 'Bet you're sorry you won!' That was very much the tone.

Play It Loud came out at the end of November 1970, but it didn't get much more attention than *Beginnings* had, and that was a disappointment. We knew we weren't quite there, but we hoped that it would do better than it did. We'd tried the skinhead experiment and that hadn't worked either, so we were feeling a bit unsure of things.

Around that time I remember us seeing the Move at Walsall town hall, and they all had on these coloured suits.

Roy Wood was sat on the floor cross-legged and played the sitar, and we thought, *Cor, this is a pretty serious group!* They had an impact on us, and we'd already done a Jeff Lynne song from the Idle Race, 'Knocking Nails Into My House' on *Beginnings*.

Then we saw Mott the Hoople at the Wolverhampton Civic. We were a little bit gobsmacked honestly. We didn't normally all go out together to watch a band, but we went to that and they looked great. They had this slightly hippy thing going where they had their trousers tucked into knee-length boots, which was unusual because mostly back then it was flares down over your shoes. I picked up on that and then developed it a bit further – I had a pair of boots that laced right up to the top.

It wasn't just the look though; they sounded great. They had this really powerful bass drum sound – I think it was miked up to come through the PA, which was new to us. Overall, they had this very thick, strong sound which really impressed us. I called a band meeting at Dad's house and said, 'We've got to get amps like that – we need to get that sound.' We got in touch with a company called SNS and tried their amps out in a rehearsal, and it was great, much denser, a bit like Bad Company, and we ended up working with them. That boosted us, and that was important because I think we'd been feeling a bit left behind.

We needed a hit.

9

TOP OF THE POPS, HERE WE COME...

We'd reached the spring of 1971. We'd been playing together as a band in one form or another for five years, we'd made a couple of albums, got good management in Chas Chandler, but still it wasn't quite happening for us. We weren't getting desperate exactly, but we knew we needed a break somewhere.

Looking back, it was obvious really. We were a great live band, we had a good following in the clubs, we always went down a storm. So why not play to our strengths with the next single and make a record that sounded like we did on stage? We hadn't got anything of our own, so Chas suggested we try 'Get Down And Get With It', something Little Richard had done. It always went down well live with the boot-stomping, so why not do that and give ourselves a bit of a writing credit for what we'd done with it as well?

Not that we saw it then, but it was the perfect song for us, almost the template for what Slade would go on and do. It had a pop sensibility about it, and then on top of that there was this driving, rock element. It wasn't blended, they were just one on top of the other, the contrasts rubbing up against each other, and that was the style that we really did begin to mine from there.

From the minute Nod opened his mouth with 'Well all right!' that was Slade, all that energy, the attack that we had as a live act. It wasn't soft plectrums, it was hard, like you're putting your shoulder into it. It was all that Brummie flailing hair and the knee that goes in and out. We were moving, that was what we'd captured on record for the first time. It's not like you could just stand there and play Slade music, you had to throw yourself into it, and we finally started getting that across. Everything was suddenly to do with creating an atmosphere, making it feel live, even if more controlled in the studio.

Those listening to the record were now able to get a sense of what our audience felt in the clubs, because when people are watching you and you're engaging in the power of it, it just wallops them, you can feel them being driven by it. The song had a bloody good guitar sound, and when I was playing it, there was a real blokey thing about it, some sort of force, like rock 'n' roll in its early days had, with Chuck Berry or whoever. The guitars were quite cutting as well. They weren't soft and bloated, they were a driving force; suddenly they were jumping out of the speakers at you.

Then on top of that, you've got Nod bawling away! That became his sound from there on, on records as well as live, and it gave us a character of our own, made us instantly recognisable. But what was lovely about the record is that it was about the band, about what we were, who we were. We didn't mess about with it in the studio, we just went in and knew we had to make it sound live, like we were playing it in a club, make it sound the way the audience heard it.

We made the recording, but it hadn't quite got the atmosphere and there were some bits of wood lying around from a platform where a drum kit had stood, so we started stamping on this wood and clapping, the kind of noise you get from a crowd stamping their feet. That was the forerunner to what we did on 'Coz I Luv You'. Chas thought it could do with a bit of rock 'n' roll piano as well, so he got Zoot Money to come down, which was good. It didn't take over, it just added to it. Once we had the finished record, we knew we had caught what we were about at last, and we just wanted other people to hear it.

It came out at the start of June, and of course we didn't know how it was going to go. I think it was John Peel who played it, and we were driving down Edgware Road in London. We pulled over at the sound of, 'This is from a new band, Slade...' – this was in the days when you could park in London! We sat there listening to it and knew that at last we had the right record. The excitement of listening to it, that was great. It's not like it had loads of airplay, but you could feel the momentum coming. From gigging up and down the country, we had built that base of people who would buy our record when it came out, our core fans. From there, the trick was to get it on

Radio 1, because that was a national station. That play on Radio 1 covered the country.

It got in the charts in the first week at forty-five, then went up to forty-two. We had been with Polydor for some time at this point without having a hit, and so the issue now was would this record get into the top forty and get us on to *Top of the Pops*? I remember waiting in Robert Stigwood's office. Chas was in there, and I remember seeing Ginger Baker knocking about. I'll never forget the anticipation as we waited for the chart to come out. There was a park outside Stigwood's office, and we were all just wandering around it and then we went back to the office. There was a real nervousness. All we needed to do was go up a few places and then *Top of the Pops* would take us.

We broke into the top forty at thirty-two and then on 15 July 1971, when we were up to twenty-nine, we went on *Top of the Pops*, and that really was the start of something else, the next phase for Slade.

For the show I wore a boiler suit because Pete Townshend was wearing them at the time and I got a designer version of one. I had mine in orange, all the one colour because Chas was very clear that having one colour worked, it made a statement, and he was right about that. I had my boiler suit fitted with diamonds sewn into the trousers and wore a woman's pink coat. I had the long hair with the fringe going again by then as well. I think Marc Bolan probably had an influence on me, but I took it to where I wanted to take it.

I'd wear women's coats because they were long and made me seem a bit taller. A bit later I got a silver coat that became really well known, made by somebody in London. I'd got this idea, it must have been from somebody off the TV, that silver looked really good on black and white TV, which most people still had at the time. Then there were the lace-up boots to the knee, which we'd taken from Mott the Hoople.

From that idea came the platforms. I got a pair of platform boots with a stripe down the side from a woman's shoe shop in Walsall. After that I went to London, to Kensington Market, where there were lots of individual stallholders who used to make things for people – I got the boiler suit from there actually, from Mr Freedom. You'd walk round there and it always stank of dope or essence of petunia. That's where Freddie Mercury was working at the time, making shoes and hats. I didn't know him, but he was there.

Something was cooking, and I seemed to be the chef. I was the one making a statement about the way we looked, and it all seemed to make sense. That's something that I've always had somehow, even now. I can go shopping, and I'll put a top hat or something on my head and ask people if it looks silly and the reply is always, 'It doesn't look silly on you!' Somehow with clothes I just know, it's instinctive, it's intuitive. I think it goes back to growing up in that black and white kind of England after the war and wanting a bit of colour, that burst of Max Miller from the music hall. I wanted to make people smile, give them something larger than life, entertain them.

That was very much my role in things, to catch the eye, and on that appearance on *Top of the Pops*, it was all personally home-made stuff that I tarted up: a girl's coat, trousers, boots. Thinking about the four of us, there was always a lot of energy, but Don and Nod, they couldn't move about much, Don behind his kit and Nod with the microphone. Nod hadn't got the glitzy top hat idea yet either, he was more of a Jack the Lad, a working-class look with his huge flat cap and sideboards. Then you had Jim, who looked a bit more serious, so it fell to me to make the show, I suppose.

It did the trick, because I remember the reaction from people was all, 'Did you see Slade on TV?' On *Top of the Pops* we were the show with the New Seekers, Labi Siffre, Curved Air, the Dave Clark Five and Middle of the Road. There was nothing like us. Nothing. That was the start of the real breakthrough for us.

We were on the programme three times in total over the following few weeks as the single got up to number sixteen. *Top of the Pops* also had a video company which did promotional things, and they said they could do with a video from us. So we went to Battersea Power Station and got on the roof, and you can see Nod bellowing the song out. In reality, all we were doing was recreating the scene in *A Hard Day's Night* when the Beatles escaped from the theatre and were all running around. It was so exciting, it was nothing but fun, until I got on a ledge and looked down and then I just froze – I was scared of heights!

10

NUMBER ONE

We'd got a top twenty but that wasn't the end of the journey – we'd only really just got the show on the road, overnight successes after five years of trying!

'Get Down And Get With It' had four weeks in the top twenty and nearly three months in the top forty, and Chas said we needed to get another single out to capitalise on it. The obvious initial thought was another rock record, but we came up with 'Coz I Luv You', which was very different in sound.

'Coz I Luv You' started off as a bit of a jam between Jim and Don, Don playing a rhythm with a straight bass drum, and Jim on the violin. I think it came together when we were down at some old church in Wednesbury. We used to rent it from a vicar who used to come down to the pub! Jim was playing this thing with Don, and we were bringing in a couple of influences from elsewhere with the violin – Marc Bolan was in mind, Curved Air possibly too. Jim was always very good at remembering something, and he went away and told Nod about the idea, and the two of them got the song together pretty quickly. That was really the start of their songwriting partnership.

It wasn't necessarily our first choice as a follow-up. I remember we'd heard Emperor Rosko on the radio saying we needed another rocker, and we had that in mind. He was a DJ, he must know what he was talking about! We liked the song but it sounded a bit lightweight in comparison to the previous one when we finished it. But Chas recognised something in it straight away. He loved it, he knew this was a big hit. His logic was absolutely cock on, and I'm not going to argue with a man who proved himself right! He thought that the change of pace would be perfect.

We recorded it at Olympic Studios, and with the violin and the bits of lead that I was playing, we were going off in a new direction. It was really happening for us. We were getting happier in the studio, we were working on our own material, we were all able to bring something of ourselves to the song, and at the recording. I remember feeling really good about things when we recorded it. Then Chas went away and mixed it and got us all into the office in London to play it. It was different to how we had imagined, but we didn't take that much convincing because I think we quickly saw that he was right. I remember sitting there, and it was like that feeling when you are trying to deny something that you know is right – what's the point? Chas had real conviction about it.

The stomping and the clapping made it a very different record to anything else that was out there. The boot-stomping gave it an identity, and the offbeat clapping was another twist – that was me in the corridor mucking around when we were trying to work out how we were going to do it. Chas heard it, got all of us to do that *bap-bap* really quick, went in and double-tracked it, and then we had something that was so simple but so big.

It wasn't an out-and-out rock song, but it wasn't lightweight either. The violin had a part in that too. Jim played more of a rock violin, a bit of a harder edge to it, staccato, like a marching song. That contrasted with Nod singing differently to how he had on 'Get Down And Get With It'. That was a really raucous vocal, where this was a bit softer. There were these contrasts rubbing up against each other all over the record, and they just worked.

As a recording, it was undeniably right, it had something special. And then there was the title. The words were spelled 'wrong', but the kids got it straight away. It was something they could identify with, they talked the same way. The fact that it was very different to the last single as well, that opened things up for us. It wasn't an obvious rock record, but it still had a real power to it. That is so important because without a good song, without a good record, you've got nothing, certainly not over the long term. You can't see a band on the radio, so you sell a record by making it a good song in the first place. Then anything else you can add to it on stage or on TV to make it better, that's a bonus.

I remember we met Polydor in Park Lane. Chas played them the record, and right away there was a real buzz, they were really excited, there was a strong feeling about it right from the off, and then it started to get a lot of airplay too. We needed that, it took us up another level. 'Get Down And Get With It' had opened the door, it had got us on radio and television, people had seen what we looked like, they were intrigued, but we hadn't cracked it by any means. But that next song was going to push us through the door and out into centre stage.

It was the speed at which the record moved that was amazing. It went in at twenty-six and *Top of the Pops* played it at the start with the crowd dancing to it, then it was up to number eight in the second week, our first top ten. I was at the Inn on the Park, just down from Marble Arch, and there was a reception as Chas was re-signing the band to Polydor. The Inn on the Park was a posh hotel and we were working-class blokes who couldn't afford posh hotels. The record had a strong chance of getting to number one. And then it did! I still remember the excitement. Even back in Wolverhampton people sat up and took notice. That led to having our photograph being taken on the top of the Mander Centre, the main shopping mall in town. That was special, magic. People still tell me where they were when they first heard that record.

We had always been confident about it because people around us really took to it, they saw it as a step up. Quite often family and friends were our jury, helping make decisions on what we should release. Chas always made a point of getting us to take the acetates home to play to them, because they were the kind of people who would give you the most honest answer. With 'Coz I Luv You', my sister Carol never had any doubts that it was going to be a big hit. She tells the story better than me...

Dave had been in groups for years, I just took it for granted, but the possibilities of just what he was involved in didn't really hit me until November 1971, when 'Coz I Luv You' came out. There was a beat in that song that was something different, something unique, and that was when I knew Slade were going to be really big, when I first heard that. When Dave played me the acetate demo disc of it, straight away I said, 'That'll be number one.' It made the hairs stand up on the back of my neck.

I was a rep at the time, and every Tuesday we'd meet in Birmingham at lunchtime to pass our samples over. In 1971 Tuesday lunchtime was when they announced the charts on Radio 1. They'd have the rundown, going up and up the charts, starting at number forty, and then at one o'clock they'd announce the number one.

So I was sitting in the car with the radio tuned in, eating my sandwiches, and I told all the other reps, 'I'm not talking to you lot, I'm listening to the charts. I've got to see where my brother is.'

'Coz I Luv You' had gone in at twenty-six, and then gone up to number eight. So the countdown went on. Number twenty, number fifteen, number ten, no mention, so at least it hadn't gone down.

Eight, seven, six, five, still nothing. The others are looking at me through the car window, they're listening as well, and they're all making faces, saying, 'He's been knocked off the charts!' But I knew that hadn't happened. You don't go up to eight and then disappear out of the top forty altogether the next week.

Number four, nothing. Three, nothing. Then he played number two. And it wasn't Slade. And I got out of the car and I felt sick. I said, 'He's number one!' The other reps they picked me up and threw me in the air – me in my miniskirt! I had to go home. I couldn't do anything, I was a wreck.

I came back home to Mom and Dad's house in Penn, and eventually Dave walked in the house. 'Can I please come to *Top of the Pops?*'

'You can come where you like, but you'll have to get yourself there.'

Looking back, I still can't believe it really. I got to the BBC studios and there's Marc Bolan's Rolls-Royce in the car park. I went into reception and was ushered away to the dressing room. I felt like royalty! I was always a dancer and Dave said, 'Do you want to go and watch Pan's People rehearse?' Pan's People? These faultless, glorious girls? Me, watching them rehearse?

So I was putting some lipstick on in the mirror to go and see Pan's People and in walks this bloke. I see him through the mirror and I'm thinking, *Wow, I fancy him!* He'd got two bottles of champagne behind his back, but we could all see these bottles in the mirror. He was chatting away, really pleased for them that they were successful, handing this champagne out, and I'm thinking, *When he's gone, I'm going to find out who he is!*

So he walked out, and I looked across at Dave and said, 'Wow!'

He said, 'You can forget it, he won't fancy you.'

It was Elton John!

Top of the Pops played a massive part in our success, but it was something we were very nervous about back then. They had all these funny little rules because of the unions at the time, and at that point you had to have some part of the performance that was live – it couldn't just be the record – and that scared us to death because the record sounded great, so different. We were worried we'd lose that on *Top of the Pops* because that was the most important showcase you had at the time.

In the finish we had to provide them with the backing track to the record but take the vocal out, so Nod had to go out there and sing live on *Top of the Pops*, which was big pressure for him. Nod did a good job, but we were concerned because Nod had got this real good vocal sound together in the studio and we weren't sure it would come across the same. But Nod was great, we came across really well, and the rest is history.

Then we started going on a lot of TV shows, and for the most part you used to mime to the record, and there were some really terrible people at doing that at the time! Chas was professional about that, really disciplined with us, and made sure we did it properly, and that was a big positive for us.

Top of the Pops could be a long day. You always needed a run-through first so they could work out the cameras and the angles. You'd walk on and play, and they'd watch what you were doing, decide how to shoot it. It was a very small studio, nothing like how it looked on TV. They would have you do a dress rehearsal and then you got the rest of the day free, which was a right bore. We'd go to the canteen and then I'd probably go up Kensington Market, buying clothes.

We got on the show more and more often, and I had to wear something different every time, that was part of the excitement of it, the theatre. Even the band didn't know what I'd come up with a lot of the time. They'd be in the dressing room and it'd be, 'Where's H?' 'He's in the toilet getting dressed!'

Did I hide what I was wearing? Oh yes, partly to surprise them and partly because I wasn't always sure they'd approve, especially Jim, who didn't seem so keen on that aspect of it. It wasn't so bad with 'Coz I Luv You' because we were all wearing long coats, and I'd already worn one on stage and we'd got an idea of what we were going to do. We planned that. The hairstyles and the long coats were basically what we were doing on stage, although it got a bit wilder later on!

It was a strange time looking back. We had a number one record; we'd go and play it on *Top of the Pops* and then I'd come home to the council house and the box room, living with Mom and Dad, and all this time me and Jan were going out with each other. That was good for me, I think, it kept my feet firmly on the ground. People also thought we were all millionaires, but I can promise you we weren't! Chas would finance certain things for the publicity side and so on, and we just went home and the money would come when the money came. I don't think anybody made any particular changes in the first year at all.

We were still playing the Queen Mary Ballroom, the odd working men's club. We weren't doing big gigs. We hadn't stepped further into that, into theatre tours. You can have a number one, a hit record, but it doesn't mean you're going to sell out the Birmingham Odeon. It wasn't like that. In fact we were still playing to fifty people. A lot of people didn't know we had a number one; the people following us weren't always into that kind of thing. I remember we went across to Europe for a few days at the end of November to do some television stuff, then we came back, and December 1971 was the first real step in terms of gigs, because we played a number of colleges and town halls, and the college circuit especially was really important at that point.

I think it was after 'Coz I Luv You' that I received my first royalty cheque for £1,000. I added £200 to it and went out and bought a Jensen. That was quite a bit of money in the early seventies, but I don't remember anything phenomenal being paid to me. I certainly don't recall ever being rolling in it, but I don't remember ever being concerned about it either. To me I was doing something I loved. I had been doing it a long time, I was getting paid a bit better for it at last, and I didn't get concerned about what lay ahead of me. We trusted Chas, and we got into a routine: the next date came along in the studio, we recorded two or three songs, the single was chosen. There was a rota for gigging, studio, possible holiday, gigging.

As we got into 1972, that was when you could really feel the change happening for us in terms of gigs, and we did drive ourselves really hard that year. I remember somebody saying later that Chas was making sure we didn't have any time off so we didn't have the time to complain about working so hard, and there might be a bit of truth in that.

Chas's thinking was that the country was still looking for the next Beatles, there was a very definite sense of that. The talk in the music press was always about them re-forming or, if not, who would replace them. Chas was convinced it was going to be us because we had a lot more cooking in the kitchen than most bands. A lot of bands relied on writers but we had a lot of versatility in Slade. We had two excellent writers who were starting to come to the fore, we had musical styles where all of us were bringing something different in, we had distinct personalities, so there were different things for different fans to pick up on. Plus there were four of us, and, as the Beatles had proved, visually that was really strong – to have three guitar players in the front line rather than adding a singer who stood there without an instrument or a keyboard player stuck behind a piano or an organ. Four is a good number for photos too, you can do a lot with four people. There was no waste in the group, nothing spare – it was all there, focused. I always remember Chas saying, 'People are looking for the new Beatles. Here they are!' That's what he believed. He wanted us to have waxworks at Madame Tussauds.

I think also in our favour was that we were a band who were very much about having a good time, about enjoying yourself, and that was important in a country where things weren't going that great economically. There was a miners' strike for a couple of months early in 1972, there were power cuts; it was all a bit depressing and we were a bit of an antidote to that. We were colourful, we were funny, a bit daft – me especially – we made people smile, and that was something different at a time when music had gone very serious with people like Led Zeppelin, Black Sabbath, progressive rock and all of that. We were a good-time band, and people needed that. I think Chas saw all of that a lot more clearly than we did. He saw that we'd got through the door with 'Coz I Luv You', and he was going to make sure we kept it open.

He kept us focused and worked us hard. We had a few days off at Christmas to celebrate the success we'd had and then we just tore into 1972. Aside from recording, doing press and TV and all of that, we played over 160 gigs that year, mostly in Britain, with a few in Europe. We also had our first taste of America too, and that was crazy. We played our first show in San Diego on 3 September, came back to do a gig in London on the 7th and another in Weston-Super-Mare on the 9th, then we were in Las Vegas on the 10th!

Somehow we found time to write and record some material as well, and again Chas had been very shrewd. As 'Coz I Luv You' was being released, he booked us in for three gigs at a small place in Piccadilly in London to make a live album. We did it with 300 people off the street, pulled in to come and have a laugh! We needed an audience, and they just went along with it. We had to enhance that by going in the corridors and clapping to overdub onto it!

I think Chas reckoned that if we were going to be as big as he thought, we'd struggle to find the time to make a proper LP early in '72, especially as he wanted us to keep on banging out the singles and he didn't want those to go on the LP – that was very much the way back then, something the Beatles had pioneered. But he also knew we needed to put an album out because a lot of the singles buyers would be after one, and he didn't want them buying *Play It Loud* because that was associated with the skinhead thing. It was really clever, and it was good to know that we had that live album up our sleeve to release when the time was right.

That came after we'd released our follow-up single, 'Look Wot You Dun'. This was a bit different again, a bit rockier this time, using piano instead of the violin to give it a different character. There was a chance for me to play a nice solo in the middle eight, and the whole thing had that kind of sound that Lennon had at the time. It was a good record, but probably not as instant as 'Cos I Luv You'. It got to number four and stuck there for three weeks, so that established us as a hit factory.

Then, just as that started to drop down the charts, we released *Slade Alive!* to keep us right in people's faces. It was a bit of a retro album, very much more the way we'd been prior to having the hits, and again Chas's timing was spot on. Twelve months before, we'd only been known as a live band, but after three hits we suddenly had fans who didn't know that side of us. That album really showcased the other side of us and did us a lot of good, especially as it came out in March, just before the festival gigs started to come round. It was a great calling card for us in that respect. It sold really well, got to number two and was in the charts for well over a year.

Saying that, we were a bit disappointed that 'Look Wot You Dun' hadn't been as big a hit as we'd hoped, so as the live album was released we had two days in the studio to cut some new tracks. Chas wanted us to get back to that straight beat again, and 'Take Me Bak 'Ome' was right on the money. It had real power to it, Nod's vocal just got the hairs up on the back of the neck, it had those elements that were becoming the classic Slade sound.

It came out in the week that we played the Lincoln Festival over spring bank holiday at the end of May. This wasn't our crowd at all; it was very much an albums-oriented thing. Acts like the Groundhogs, Humble Pie, the Strawbs, Genesis, Rory Gallagher were on, and if you were having hits, it was seen as a bit of a sell-out. We got booed when we went on, but we absolutely stormed it, and by the end they were all over us. That backed up the reputation the live album was getting us, and suddenly we were attacking on two fronts. We were a proper rock band but we were having huge hit singles as well.

That summer, we played in Germany, France, Finland, Spain, Belgium, laying down some groundwork in Europe which, years later, would really do us good when the hits dried up a bit in the UK. We also played some smallish gigs over here, fulfilling bookings that we'd made before we started having hits, and that was difficult sometimes because too many people wanted to get in.

'Take Me Bak 'Ome' was in the charts all summer, along with the live album – the other two albums got back in the charts as well on the back of that – and we were becoming really big, but then at the start of September we moved into a completely different league when we released 'Mama Weer All Crazee Now'. Straight in at number two, then a number one for three weeks, it was massive, tipping things towards hysteria wherever we went.

As the years go by, you come to realise that timing is really important in life, and in 1972 and into '73 we were the right band doing the right thing in the right place at the right time. I've already mentioned these were grim times, and a lot of kids used our records to lighten that gloom, but more than that, colour tellies were starting to appear in more and more living rooms, and if ever a band was made for colour television, it was us!

We took complete advantage of that – me especially – by wearing more and more colourful clothes every time we were on *Top of the Pops*. We were characters. If you'd wanted to make a cartoon at the time, we would have been ideal. You could pick on features and people would remember you – my peculiar hairstyle, something like that. Reeves and Mortimer picked that up years later, especially with me and Nod, who were the obvious ones.

I loved being on television and having the chance to show off. I didn't have any qualms about it. I would poke my nose into every angle of the camera because Nod would get more shots than me, and I was like that because my job was to entertain people, give them a good time. I was the joker. Over the years people have come up to me so many times and said, 'I'll always remember that *Top of the Pops*,' or, 'We tuned in to see what daft costume you would have on,' or whatever. Chas always encouraged me, he was never negative. He wanted me to have a silver wig or the biggest platform boots.

Every time we went on *Top of the Pops* I had to have something different to wear. Later on I had a couple of designers making all my stuff, but then I'd buy stuff in shops and boutiques. It wasn't always easy going into a shop in Walsall to buy a woman's blouse, so I ended up shopping in London! That really excited me, the colours and Carnaby Street, all of that. I suppose it was a reaction to the years of being told what to do and what to wear at school and at Tarmac.

It did have its downside though. When we'd had a couple of hits, I met somebody from my school class in a local pub, the Dutchman, at the back of the youth centre. He was going, 'Buy me a drink.' It was a bit hostile. He was saying, 'Why do you wear those peculiar clothes?' He didn't get it. That started to happen a lot to us. *Top of the Pops* meant I was so famous I had to stop going into ordinary places. A lot of the time it was nice, but there'd be blokes like him who would be watching the TV on Thursday in the pub, and I might be in there too because it was recorded, not live. He couldn't see me as the kid he went to school with. He saw me on TV, and I looked odd. Also I was having success, and he couldn't handle it.

But the success just kept coming, so much so that we now really did need a new LP just to keep up with the demand. *Slayed?* came out in November, and I remember it as a good collection of songs, most of them by Jim and Nod together, one each on their own and a couple of covers. It was a good example of what we were like at the time, the way we worked. Jim tended to come in with the chords and the structure of the song, and then we would play through it in different ways and after the four of us had worked that way, we'd get in the studio with Chas and record things.

It was very interesting how it all worked out. We were almost battling with each other, but battling in a nice way. Some bass players play behind the beat, whereas Jim was always slightly ahead, and often that was the excitement of the tracks. We were putting down the basic track; Nod would be in a booth so you could hear his voice but he would have his guitar on, and Chas would be in the control room at the top, so you could see him. By now these were songs we were writing for recording, not for the live act like we had in the early days, so we would still be piecing bits together because we hadn't done them live.

To get the real vibe we would do it several times and never go for the first take. That was dangerous because you can lose some of that early excitement, but we were still pretty quick in turning things round and Chas was great at getting that live feel. He didn't stifle the sound, he kept it simple and opened it up. He could have said, 'What we need to do is to add this, and then add that, and add this,' but that wasn't his style. Where he was great was that he heard what we had and could see how it would be played live. He wouldn't ask for three guitars, he wanted to keep the integrity of us as a live band.

When you're in the studio you have headphones on, so you aren't hearing the amplifiers as such, they're all screened off. You're hearing a mix in your cans, but you're looking at each other, so you're still very much a group. Don was usually on a riser, we were all around. I remember clearly that Nod only had his headphones on one ear and left the other one off. We would do one take and then Chas would say, 'Right, come on,' and we would all go up and have a listen and then go back and do some more. It was a really exciting process but scary as well because you can be doing the track and it comes to the point where it's really cooking and you're hoping no one ruins it!

Don was great in the studio. He'd hardly ever make a mistake because he was great at grabbing something, he knows intuitively about rhythm. He's not a complicated drummer, it's a root thing, but he can hold it. He'd be the glue and we'd add things around him. It's about listening to each other, watching each other, feeding off each other.

With Jim's style of bass playing you don't want a complicated lead, so my playing was about feel. I always go cold when guitarists talk of the mix. Talking about things technically just wasn't my thing, and Chas was very much the same. He wasn't into bullshit. People would talk to him about Hendrix and be academic about it, about him playing a pentatonic on a flat and fifth, and Chas would tell them where to go. Hendrix might have been playing a pentatonic on a flat and fifth but Chas didn't need to be told that. I understand that I play some of those things naturally, and I think with Slade there was a lot of playing without it being academically worked out. I could play because I'd been listening to great records for years and getting my education that way, not through lessons. Chas grasped that and he was always really encouraging about my playing. In Slade you will hear my guitar quite loud, but then you have all this ringing going on, which is very much to do with early Beatles, obviously a big influence on me. I would also bring a twist to it. It's a matter of drive and the human power behind it. I was ambitious, I wanted us to be successful, I was having a great time, and all that energy, that enthusiasm, that joy, it came out in the way I played.

I think we caught a lot of that on *Slayed?* even if by then we had to include 'Mama Weer All Crazee Now' on it to keep the record company happy. It was a defining record for us, not least because of the sleeve, which has become iconic for us. We did the photo shoot with Gered Mankowitz again, and he was great at being fed an idea and finding some way of realising it.

Chas always had the idea that the group would be more successful if it was all about Slade the group, not us as individuals, so he didn't want our names on the cover; he wanted us to be a four-headed creature. That was where us all having slade written on our fists came from. Chas said, 'Stick your thumbs out and you've got S L A D E,' though Don had plasters on two fingers. Gered had to work all afternoon to get that one shot. I stripped off because I was muscly and it showed a tougher side of things, and that started the move towards me becoming known as Super Yob, I suppose. Funny that the one who was known for his way-out clothes was the one with his top off. I think the cover gave us a harder edge than people might have thought we had as a singles group. It built on what we'd done at the Lincoln Festival and again it gave us a foot in two markets, rock and pop.

As I've said, we headed out to America in September 1972 to dip our toes in the water over there. We even took our own fans with us! We'd organised a competition for a fan to design the sleeve of *Slade Alive!*, and the prize was to come out to the States with us. So we were playing these massive venues like the Spectrum in Philadelphia, supporting Humble Pie in front of crowds who had no idea who we were, and at the front there were a few people going mental!

They stood out a mile because the American audience were stoners, sitting cross-legged on the floor and rolling up joint after joint. We didn't fit into that scene because we didn't do drugs. Apart from smoking a bit of pot like probably everybody did, there was nothing else – and I wasn't really any good at that either! There were always drugs around us but we weren't taking them, certainly not coke or heroin or any of that stuff. We didn't seem to need it.

Maybe it was just our attitude towards things. We were always a bit grounded. We didn't want to be a group that chucked tellies out of the window or wrecked bedrooms. I suppose we had got certain principles. We worked at the job, and we kept our heads clear. We weren't turning up drunk at recording sessions. We understood the importance of getting the job done and appreciated the opportunity we had earned for ourselves. My growing up was done on the Warstones council estate, and the other lads came from similar stock.

We found it hard to spend money because we knew the value of it. I don't think I did anything particularly wild with money. I spent a bit on stage clothes – that was nothing unusual – but the money came in slowly anyway. It was twelve months until we started to see something. That's normal because record royalties do come in late.

However, Chas would always advise us not to go cheap, and he was right about that. We were staying at a hotel in Sussex Gardens in London for a fiver a night, and a record company executive came over from America and we took him back there. We were sitting in our room with him, discussing going over to America, and I don't imagine we made the best impression.

But anyway, America could wait. First, we were going to finish conquering the UK...

11

1973 – TRIUMPHS AND TRAGEDIES

We kept the pot boiling at the end of 1972 by releasing 'Gudbuy T'Jane' in November, and it got to number two, kept off the top by Chuck Berry of all people with 'My Ding-A-Ling'. I suppose that was fair enough considering how much we'd all listened to him when we were younger! We played a big UK tour through November and into the start of December as well, and then we had a few weeks off over Christmas to prepare for the following year, which we knew was going to be really important for us – 1972 was the last year when Slade didn't play a big part in Christmas, as it turned out!

Although we hadn't made it a hat-trick of number ones, we weren't worried because we knew we had something special ready for the start of the new year. We released 'Cum On Feel The Noize' at the end of February and were very confident we had a real hit on our hands, though I don't think even we were prepared for just what a huge success it was going to be. It went straight in at number one, the first time that had happened since the Beatles released 'Get Back', so that was the final seal of approval on Slademania, to do something they'd done. That felt huge.

How we worked at that time was like this. Jim and Nod would come in with a song, 'this is how it goes', which was a great feeling because we wouldn't know the song when it arrived, it was a fresh tune. We hadn't got a demo to listen to and figure out what I was going to play. No, they'd just turn up. Nod would sing it, then you'd roll over it several times and Don and I would add our things to it and make it work as a band. 'Cum On Feel The Noize' was never played live before we recorded it, and I think the excitement that you get as a musician, working something up for the first time, comes through on the record. We hadn't played it to death on the road, it was fresh out of the box, and it's got that electricity as a result.

In its way, I think it was the perfect example of what Chas recognised that night when he saw us in Rasputin's for the first time. He immediately picked up on our personalities and the excitement we generated, on how different we were. He always said we played different chords from other rock 'n' roll bands, who were more obvious in their structures – twelve bars and things like that. Most rock records use major chords, which are generally very up and rocky, unlike the minor Tamla Motown chords. But 'Cum On Feel the Noize' is a major/minor thing, the kind of trick a lot of very successful songwriters use a lot. The best way I can sum it up is to quote that line 'but how strange the change, from major to minor' from the Cole Porter song, 'Ev'ry Time We Say Goodbye'. That change gives the song a bittersweet feel. There's a happiness to it as well as a melancholy, and those contrasts work so well together.

Top of the Pops for 'Cum On Feel The Noize' was a riot because I moved the clothes up a notch again. The others were waiting for me in the dressing room when I came out of the toilet in the metal nun outfit, which sent them into spasms. It was a step up from the silver coat and the glitter on the face! Nod was OK with it all because he was equally flamboyant in his own way, he had the mirrors on his top hat and all that, and Chas loved it, he could see that what I was doing was helping us get on television. We were a very visual act as well as a musical one, and the more TV exposure we got, the more records we sold.

Some could say people didn't notice how good we were musically because of the clothes we wore, and the look of the band was a huge part of what we were about. But in that period when we were having the hits, everything came together just right and the music fed the clothes, the clothes fed the exposure, which fed back to the music. It was a virtuous circle, all about the sum of the parts creating something special. I'm short and was always looking for something to make me bigger, so platform soles were something that appealed and they had become a bit of a trademark. But they also needed the right sort of clothes, long coats and that kind of thing. The fact that I was slim, plus the way we were shot on TV, meant that I came across as being quite tall.

Talking of clothes, there were a few hilarious moments with feathers and capes that I remember. One costume looked like fish scales and was really bizarre. Those moments took me back to when I wore a weird hat and a cape and walked through Woolworths in Wolverhampton, just looking at people watching me, long before we got famous. I had done that to get a reaction, and so to get an opportunity to do it on television was just great.

'Cum On Feel The Noize' underlined that we were the most popular band in the UK at the time, and when we announced a UK tour in June, we sold out town halls and the like all over the country. The only way we could accommodate the demand was to play a huge gig somewhere, so we booked a show at Earl's Court in London on 1 July 1973.

At that stage nobody had played there – Bowie did a show there after we booked ours – so it was a real unknown quantity. It held 20,000 people, five or six times bigger than any of the theatre gigs that we played. It was a bit of a gamble in a lot of ways, but Chas was confident we could sell it out, no problem, and as usual he was right. We were out of the country when tickets went on sale, we had a month in America, but when we came home, you could smell something in the air. We were everywhere, it was getting hysterical, you couldn't imagine how it could get any bigger.

The week of the Earl's Court gig, we released 'Skweeze Me Pleeze Me', and it flew out of the shops. We sold 300,000 in that first week, and it went straight in at number one. We'd got the Midas touch. Then we were into the gig and it was crazy. The Tubes were full of kids all wearing glitter, top hats, the full works, who piled into this huge place. Like an aircraft hangar it was, but it felt like everybody was at a massive party. It came across as really intimate considering how huge the place was. We really pulled it off. It was a very memorable night, something very special. We were on top of the world. For the moment. I'll leave the next part of the story to Carol.

In June '73 I went to Ibiza on holiday with a friend, Angela Morris, who was Don's girlfriend. While we were out there, Don rang and spoke to me and told me to shoo Angela out onto the balcony because he wanted to tell me something. She was coming up to twenty-one and he'd ordered her a pink E-Type Jaguar for her birthday. They were very much together and it was fun knowing something she didn't!

We flew back to Gatwick in the morning before the boys were playing Earl's Court that night. Don had left his Bentley at the airport for us to drive to the gig, and when we got in it, we found T-shirts draped over the driver and the passenger seats, black T-shirts with silver writing SKWEEZE ME PLEEZE ME written across the chest.

Don left her a lovely note, but he also told her that those T-shirts were our ticket into Earl's Court. We were to drive to the Holiday Inn at Swiss Cottage, leave the car and then get a taxi to the show. So Angela's twenty, driving this whacking great white Bentley with blacked-out windows. As we were driving, I could feel us drifting to the left. I got her to let go of the wheel and, sure enough, the car went left, so there was obviously a problem with it. We got to the hotel, but I told her that she needed to tell Don about it. I don't know if she ever did.

The morning after Earl's Court, Dave came to my hotel room and told me that he had a thing to do with the BBC all day, so rather than wait for him I went home on the train – he paid for the ticket and bought me lunch. I said goodbye to Angela, who was going to wait for Don, and came home. The day after, I got a message to say they were having a party in Wolverhampton that night and did I want to go, but I was just too tired. I had work the next day, so I left it.

I woke up the next morning and the phone was ringing. This was about seven o'clock, so I dashed down to get it, and it was one of the neighbours. 'Is your dad there?' So I went and got him and went back to bed. I heard him say, 'I haven't had time to talk to Carol yet,' so that got my interest straight away. I was worried it was something about Mom, because Dave had told me that while I'd been on holiday, she'd gone into hospital at Stafford again.

Dad came up with a tray of tea as usual, sat down on my bed and said, 'I've got some really sad news. Don's had a car accident, and the rumour is that his girlfriend was killed.' I remember saying, 'Angela's his girlfriend, she's all right.' I shot off downstairs and phoned her dad, and he told me she was dead. I remember I screamed.

Carol remembers that part of it better than I do. I can only vaguely remember hearing about the accident, probably because of the shock. It was a bit confusing. At the start it sounded like Don had had just a bit of a bump in the car, nothing that serious. Another call came a bit later and then everything unravelled from there. He was in a coma, he'd got broken ribs and ankles, would he survive? You couldn't really believe it had happened, you couldn't come to terms with the reality of it, and all just a couple of days after we'd had this massive triumph playing at Earl's Court. From the highest peak to the lowest low, just like that.

One of the hardest things to handle with a tragedy like that is that the world carries on around you when you don't want to be a part of it. 'Skweeze Me Pleeze Me' stayed at number one for three weeks, but after the first week obviously we weren't playing *Top of the Pops*. We couldn't. Don was lying in hospital. It was just the crowd or Pan's People dancing to it, and it was like they were in mourning. The way it was in the papers, it was like they were preparing for a state funeral or something.

The accident was blitzed across all the front pages because we were the biggest band in the country. Then there was speculation that Don wouldn't survive. Me and Don, we were the ones who had formed Slade. I'd known Don for ever. I didn't know how to react, how to cope. He was a close friend, he was a band mate, there was talk he wouldn't play again. The future of the band was at stake. There were so many different pieces to it. I think we were all wondering if that was the end of Slade, but nobody wanted to say it.

Although we might have been able to get another drummer, it wouldn't have been the same Slade because Don is unique. He has rhythm. He just has, it's natural. He isn't a schooled drummer. It's a vibe he has. It's him. I remember Chas once said to Don, 'I know you listen to John Bonham, but stop it. It's about being your own person.' Chas brought that out in all of us actually.

Don was in a very bad way, in intensive care, and I couldn't bring myself to go and see him early on, I just couldn't face it, possibly because of the memories of visiting Mom in hospital. By the time I went, he was in better shape, but there was still an issue in terms of him playing. He was in bed, wired up, his head was shaved on one side and there was a big scar – he looked damaged. He had lost his sense of taste and smell, and his memory was gone; he couldn't even remember Angela, never mind the accident, and that really did affect him. They were hard times for him, because he knew Angela's parents were suffering, yet he didn't even know who Angela was any longer. He started writing a diary to remember what it was he'd done each day to help him get through things, to remind him of what had happened. He'd wake up every day with no idea of yesterday, where he'd been, what he'd done, nothing.

Once he was able to come out with us again, we had to mind him because he would do some really strange things. The three of us had to become his support network. He was in a really bad state. He was drinking too much and would get out of control. He'd say the same thing a dozen times because he'd forgotten he'd said it, and I know he got frustrated with that. He felt people were looking at him as if he was stupid, and so we tried to arrange things to stop that happening, to keep him from being exposed to awkward situations. On stage he couldn't remember the songs. We'd introduce a song and he wouldn't know how it went until we cued him in, although once that was done, he was remarkable, he'd be straight into it, just fine.

It was an incredible time in every possible regard. Hits, huge gigs, number one singles, America, the accident – things were coming at you every minute of every day and you needed to escape occasionally. Before Don's crash, we'd been scheduled to have a couple of weeks' holiday in America, me and Jan with Don and Angela. After all that had happened I didn't want to go, but I was persuaded that I needed the break and, with Don getting better, we went to Hollywood and stayed with the record company.

Earlier that year I'd bought a house in Solihull, of which more later, but Jan was very clear that she wasn't going to move in until we were married, which I completely understood. That was very much the attitude of the time. 'Living in sin' was frowned on, but I didn't want the fans to know I was married – typical pop-star thinking. Anyway, we were in Hollywood and we were talking about it one day, and somebody suggested that we go over the border to Tijuana because, 'You can get married for thirty-five dollars and nobody knows anything about it. But it's real.'

What a bloody dump! We went to some seedy place, the most unromantic thing you could imagine, up some dodgy back street, into this building and upstairs, where this bloke appeared. 'Repeat after me… Where's the ring? OK, right. Now go down the road and get this signed to make it official.' That was it. We were married on 23 July 1973, and we still are, although it wasn't until a few years later that my accountant wrote to the Mexican government to get the documents to prove it was all above board.

I do recall that Jan was wearing white – white jeans anyway. We had a bottle of Cold Duck afterwards, sparkling red wine. Looking back, it was a bit selfish, but I was very conscious of the fans. We've always been that way in Slade, so I wanted to keep it quiet. Then I sent a telegram home to Mom and Dad. Carol picked it up and opened it. I'm sure my parents were upset at not having a wedding to go to, but as it turned out Carol got married before the end of the year, so I got away with it. I didn't really think about them to be honest. I was very blinkered in that way, totally into what I was doing at the time without thinking beyond it. I'm very much a person for living in the moment that I'm in, which is how we came to get married that way.

We had an enforced break over the summer while Don was on the mend, but in late September we got on the plane for New York to start our tour. It would last a month, followed by some dates in Europe. While we were away we released 'My Friend Stan', which sold as many copies as the other singles but only reached number two, kept off the top by 'Eye Level', which was the theme to the TV detective show *Van der Valk*.

We'd got our eyes on a Christmas single though, having missed the number one slot the year before, and also because we wanted a strong end to a year that had featured such triumph and tragedy. The song we chose came from a bit of a chance remark the previous year when Jim's mother-in-law said to him that nobody seemed to write Christmas songs anymore. That set him off. Then Nod went home to his mom and dad's one night and wrote the lyric in one go after having a few beers. And the song sounds like that – it sounds like the kind of conversation people have about Christmas over a drink, very down to earth.

Because of the problems with Don, there was no time to record it before we headed to the States, and by the time we got back home, it would have been too late to get it pressed up, released and all that, so we were stuck. Fortunately, Chas knew Record Plant studios in New York was a good place – we went back and made *Nobody's Fools* there later on – and he booked us in there to make the record before the tour started.

It was an exciting place to record. John Lennon was around at the time, and there was a lot of history to the place. I remember we used a corridor to get an echo on the vocals, and we were all stood there, surrounded by these Americans going to work in the building, watching these mad Brits singing about bloody Christmas when it was still baking hot in New York.

It was the first record we'd made where we didn't all play together. Don's memory wasn't great at that point, and it was a new song – we hadn't rehearsed it, so we were putting it together from scratch. The structure was there – we knew what we were after – but we had to build it up rather than all just get in there and play it the way we had, because Don couldn't be the foundation the way he had been. We had to layer things on tape, which was new to us. We'd always played as a band, then added a few bits or replaced something if we needed to, but we'd get the basic track with all four of us playing. Now we had to overdub the drums and build the track up in bits. This was a big change for us, and it was difficult.

Even so, we liked what we'd done. Then we were straight off on tour for a month or so, so it was the end of October before we got to hear the finished record. I remember we were in Belgium and we got a call from the Brussels office of Polydor, who wanted us to go and have a bottle of champagne with them because they'd heard the single and loved it. We were all in the office, and the head guy there, he popped the cork on a bottle, then another and another. He was playing the song, and it really sounded good after a couple of drinks!

We got back home in November, and the record company was raving about it. Radio 1 were on it, and it was already going berserk. We did a TV show called *Lift Off With Ayshea* in early December, but we didn't play the Christmas song, it wasn't out yet. Ayshea came up to us and said, 'Roy Wood and Wizzard have got this Christmas song they're doing. I think it'll be the number one at Christmas.' So we said, 'Really? We've got one of them as well.' If it hadn't been for us, Roy would probably have been number one, but at that time, nobody could compete with us. We were at the pinnacle at that point and quite probably the accident even escalated that.

When the single came out, I remember Chas calling me at home: 'Davy, are you sitting down? A quarter of a million records went out today. They've run out of records. They're having to import them!' We'd sold half a million by the end of the first week, and they were shipping them in from Germany. They had to arrange to get them pressed across Europe, it was crazy. It was like everybody in the country knew it. 'Merry Xmas Everybody' was straight in at number one again, and it carried on selling until February!

It was an amazing record because it not only lifted the band when we needed it, it did the same job for the country. It was a really happy song and one that people could relate to because it summed up what Christmas was like in Britain – how you spent it, what you did, who you were with. It wasn't schmaltzy the way they often are; it was real. It was about letting your hair down, enjoying yourself – you'd earned it after a hard year, us and the country. Everything was on a downer – power cuts, strikes, the oil crisis, all of that – and so you looked forward to Christmas as a treat to get away from it. When Nod roared, 'It's Christmas!' that was like a call to everybody to forget about everything and just enjoy the holiday. That record encapsulated all of those feelings. It was as if we were saying, 'We've all survived the year, Slade and Britain, so let's celebrate!'

Right away it became another Christmas tradition, and it has carried on for forty years since. Christmas comes, and it's all about mince pies, the lights in the shops, and that record is annihilating the airwaves again! It isn't just airplay, it's also the attention it gets through Facebook and so on: 'We're having a party and this is what we're playing.' The other comment I get a lot is, 'This is your time of year.' It's amazing that it has survived the way it has. I certainly never imagined it becoming what it has, but it ended up reinventing Christmas songs. We also probably made life harder for everybody else because after that – if you were a big singles band, you then had to have a Christmas song!

It's also gone beyond Christmas, and people want to hear it at any time of the year. Years later, at the Reading Festival on August bank holiday, the crowd did it and we just followed them. Yet it was a record of its time too. 'Look to the future' made it the perfect good-time song, the tonic that the nation needed at the end of an extraordinary year – and so did we.

We were all over the television that Christmas, and I had the Super Yob guitar and wore this black costume with silver boots and this huge silver collar on it. I remember saying, 'I think it looks Egyptian,' while Jim was saying, 'We're a serious group!' Around that time I also had some white platforms with a dollar sign down each side.

Chas looked at me and said, 'Ah, 1974...' But before that, before we really set off for America, I was setting up home in Solihull.

12

SOLIHULL, LIVING NEXT DOOR TO A GIRLS' SCHOOL

Having that run of really big hit singles starting with 'Coz I Luv You' in late 1971 changed our lives in all kinds of ways, however down to earth we were. There was only so long I could go on *Top of the Pops* and then go home to the box room in Mom and Dad's council house in Rindleford Avenue. We all were growing up, outgrowing our parents' homes, and we were starting to earn some money which needed investing too.

It was in the second half of 1972 that the idea that we should get our own places to live came up, although we were all a bit slow to move because we were happy where we were. Home was very much the Midlands, though I think Chas was keen to get us to move to London. Ultimately, Jim and Nod would look at doing that because they were the songwriters and getting the publishing royalties, so they could afford to have another place down there as well. That was out of reach for me.

Jim was the first to buy his own place, still in Wolverhampton, and Don bought a flat in Tettenhall, on the edge of town. I started looking in the area and went with an estate agent, Dave Hunt, to see one in Seisdon. He didn't hang around. He walked in and pretty much straight out again. 'Overpriced.' I looked at a few more rural places around Wolverhampton, the likes of Seisdon, Wombourne, Trysull, but I couldn't find what I wanted, so Dave suggested looking in Solihull, on the south side of Birmingham. At that time, if you were doing OK and moving up in the world, Solihull was one of the places you looked at. Sutton Coldfield was another, which is where Nod finished up buying a place.

So I drove out there with Dave; we went down a couple of nice roads, and he said to me, 'There's something nice down here, but I think it's already sold,' and we went down Brueton Avenue. It was really leafy, big trees, the works, and as we were driving down, I could see what looked like a mansion at the end and I thought, *This is a bit of all right!*

There were a lot of nice houses in the road, and we looked at the one at the bottom, next to this big manor house kind of thing, which I assumed belonged to Lord Solihull or somebody. There was a sold sign outside the house, but Dave said, 'Leave it with me,' and went to the door. 'I've got an unusual gentleman in the car. I know your house is sold but he is in the area. Do you mind if he comes and has a look? You never know, do you?' He didn't say who I was, but I got out of the car and went over. The lady looked at me and said something about me being a little bit familiar, but no more than that. She was very well spoken.

In the house there were oil paintings on the walls with lights over them, not like anything I was used to. Because I always want something great or go for something bigger – a bit like the clothes, I like everything larger than life – straight away I thought, *I fancy a piece of this!* Compared to Rindleford Avenue – not that there was ever anything wrong with that – this place was a mansion, and that appealed to me. It was full of furnishings and features we'd never had, like latticed windows, oak panelling in the dining room. They had a lot of nice stuff because they owned a furniture company in Worcester.

Then we went upstairs and she showed me the four bedrooms and an electric shower. I walked into what was one of her kids' rooms and all the walls were covered in Slade pictures! There was a picture of me on the wall, and this woman looked at the wall, then at me and did this big double-take! Her daughter was absolutely besotted with us apparently. 'I shall have to tell my husband that we have had a celebrity come to the house!'

When we went into the garden there were weeping willows and all sorts – it was just lovely. There was an acre. We left and I said to Dave, 'It's a pity it's sold.' He must have got onto the agent because suddenly I was getting a call from him asking, 'How much are you prepared to pay for it?' It ended up with me gazumping the original buyers.

Of course, once I'd agreed to do it, then all the doubts started coming up. It was a heck of a lot of money, and although I was in a very successful group, I wasn't writing the songs and the money is always in the publishing. But it was something I couldn't resist. It was like going into another world, and I found that very seductive, which is strange because I was really happy where I was.

The next thing was to get the mortgage, and mortgage companies looked on pop stars as fly-by-night types who'd have no money in twelve months' time. In the end I was put in touch with City Bank, who said they would fund the mortgage and charge £500 a month. I'd not long had my first royalty cheque, which was £1,000, so this was a big commitment. And of course, being me, I was doing all this without Jan having even seen the house, which she was understandably narked about. But I was just so motivated having seen it, I had to have it.

I needed to get some proof of earnings, and I was told that Chas's word wasn't acceptable because effectively he worked for us, though that wasn't how the relationship really worked. So I phoned the MD at Polydor, John Frewin, and because of who I was, he took the call straight away – I know Nod had the same conversation with him about the same time. 'No problem, Dave, I'll draft you a letter.' So John gave me this letter that said I'd be earning £100,000 in the following year – I wish! – and that was all sorted. But it did create a bit of a rift with Chas because he was upset that I hadn't gone to him, even though I explained why I hadn't.

To be honest, I also knew deep down that if I went to Chas, he would have tried to put me off it because he didn't want us spending that kind of money. He did say,

'Do you think you can afford that, Davy? Well, hopefully things will go well...' He might have been right to be cautious as well because, looking back on it, if we hadn't had that fantastic year in 1973, it might have been rocky financially. But we were young, we were selling records like they were going out of fashion, I was caught up in the success and when I saw the house, my attitude was, *Why not?* I'd got the Jensen, now I wanted the nice house to go with it. I didn't think long term, I must confess.

Then I had to get Jan to like it, and she was a bit stand-offish about it at first, I think because I hadn't consulted her about it. I'd already bought it. I'd already pushed the boat out. But there was something else that didn't help. It wasn't Lord Solihull living at the end of the road; it was a girls' school next door. Who buys a house next to 500 girls, never mind a pop star? It was like moving in next door to St Trinian's, but I was caught up with how much I wanted it and was a little bit stupid. I just wanted it. I wanted a better life. I just thought it would all be OK...

The thing is, when you grow up in a working-class environment, whatever ambitions you might have, I suppose it's always in your mind that the reality is you will get a normal job, work nine to five – I'd certainly had a taste of that at Tarmac. And although I'd had ambitions to do something with my music, it was more from the point of view of having freedom from Tarmac, being able to travel, being able to entertain people, which is a strain that runs through the family. Carol was the same as a dancer.

It wasn't that I really thought about success or about fame, it was more about not having to conform. Success wasn't really the motivation until maybe we got that first hit, and then I got a taste for it, and I wanted another number one and another and another because it's undeniably exciting. Perhaps that's where Jim and I differ as people, because he wasn't so keen on the limelight. He was more into the writing and recording process, whereas I was definitely into the performance aspect of it, as was Don and also Nod at the time, though that changed a bit later. For Jim, I think perhaps the performing was more something you had to do to get the songs out there to people. It was creating the songs that floated his boat more.

Nothing really prepares you for being famous or for having the kind of money it seemed like we might be earning. There wasn't any easing into it really; we went from no success to having number one hits very quickly. It was like a working-class family winning the lottery: you're not used to money and then all of a sudden it's there, but in our case we had fame too. It felt strange, I can't deny it. I loved having the money and the success, but it made me a bit uneasy too. I remember telling the previous owners of the house that I didn't feel as if I deserved it. Maybe that was a legacy from Mom, who always had that guilt: 'Do I deserve something good happening to me?'

It was a constant conflict, that guilt and the desire to enjoy things and wanting that larger-than-life existence. When we moved to Solihull, I changed the car up as well.

My brother-in-law found me a Rolls-Royce. We got it off a farmer, a nice blue and silver, but I fancied gold, so I had it resprayed and the number plate put on that I'd had on all my cars over the years – YOB1. Driving that into Solihull the first time with all the net curtains twitching, that was hilarious!

Looking back, I probably went too far from home. I was not only moving physically – about an hour away – I was moving in terms of class too, and that did make me feel uncomfortable. I did still spend a lot of time back at home in Wolverhampton, partly because of that and partly because Jan wouldn't move in until we were married. When I went back to Mom and Dad's, the contrast was stark. I was in Solihull for six months before Dad got in his car to come and have a first look. He came to the front door, I shook his hand and he said, 'Well done, son,' and I was really uncomfortable with that. Dad was never a huggy person and neither was Mom. He was recognising that I'd moved up in the world, and I felt awkward with that. Mom wasn't well then, and when she did come over, I'm not entirely sure she made the connection that this was my house.

We had the business of trying to fit in, because Solihull was a very well-to-do place then. Dennis, who I bought the house from, said we two couples should go out for a meal to celebrate. We went to the George Hotel, a notable place in Solihull. There was this waiter called Ackie who used to come over and recommend things. All of a sudden I'm thinking, *How do I fit in here?* Dennis was giving it the, 'You must know about fine wines,' and of course I was cocky: 'Yes, I know all that.' So he hands me the menu with the wine list. I see this name, Don Cortez, and I thought that sounded expensive, so I called Ackie over and ordered that and he gave me a look. He brought it over and uncorked it – or at least he made the sound with his mouth of a bottle being uncorked because it came with a flick-off plastic top. I may as well have bought it from the Spar shop on my way in! I told the band that story, and Don loved it: 'You ordering the wine, Dave? Flick-off top?!' I was trying to fit in and be clever but I wasn't knowledgeable at all. The only wine I ever drank was given to us by the record company!

My new life was completely alien in a lot of ways. I remember we were given these portable eight-track players by Polydor, and they came with a James Last tape in them of all things. I remember I was in the garden and switched this thing on, and I remember the sound wafting around as if I had gone into a different world. There were all sorts of things that I hadn't noticed before. I remember the trees at night, the stars shining through and the moon out, and there were bats flying around. When you've only had a garage and a lawn, a posh house with a mature garden is a real change in atmosphere. It was nice, but it also created a feeling in me that it wasn't real. For quite a period of time I couldn't get used to my new neighbourhood of sherry drinkers and manicured lawns. It was as if I had gone into a new world.

And then there was that posh girls' school.

You have to remember that everything we did was followed by the press, and once they heard about where

I was living, the TV got interested. I did a piece with the BBC's *Midlands Today*. There's me driving into the house in the silver Jensen, and these girls behind the hedge all screaming and shouting before I disappear into the house with the reporter. Then when I get inside, I'm ankle deep in letters and cards that the girls have pushed through the door!

When I moved in, they made an announcement at the school assembly that no one was to disturb me or knock on my door. I don't think that anyone did actually knock on the door, but they certainly smoked in my garden because I could see the smoke coming up from behind the bushes and could hear the girls giggling. I couldn't go out at lunchtime because they would be in the playground, and the tennis court was opposite one of the windows.

Actually, it wasn't the school that was the nuisance, it was the fact that everybody knew where I lived. I'd get local people turning up at the door saying, 'We've come to say hello. We understand you are a really friendly guy and like chatting to people.' I must have said something like that to the press. Jan was in the background going, 'Don't invite them in!' Then I'd get fans coming and knocking on the door so it wasn't especially private, not the way I'd imagined.

Then we had a break-in of sorts, very early on. We hadn't got much furniture and we were off on tour abroad somewhere. There was a window you could pull out, and we got back to find it had been broken. I don't think we had an alarm then; we had one fitted afterwards that was connected to the police station and would play a tape,

My maternal grandparents (*centre left*, *next to car*) with extended family. Ashridge Monument, 1928.

Dad's passport photo from when he was in Australia.

My paternal grandparents, *circa* 1920s.

Dad and mom, in the garden of our council house in Warstones.

Jean Bibby, my half-sister.

Christine, me and my sister Carol, 1953.

Flete Castle, my birth place.

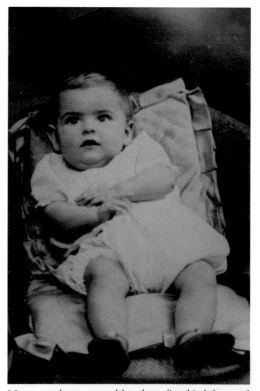

Me, around one year old and my first birthday card, which I still treasure.

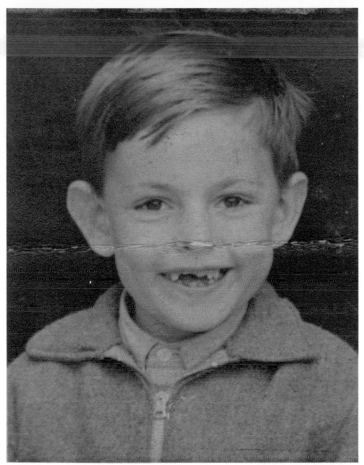

I've always been a great smiler. All I wanted for Christmas was my two front teeth...

At Jean, my half-sister's wedding. I'm third from left at the front and seem to be contemplating my next escapade!

The 'N Betweens' promo card.

The Vendors. Now it's all beginning to happen.

Real name: David John Hill
Birthdate: 4th April, 1946
Personal points: Brown hair,
   brown eyes; height 5ft. 6in.
Instruments played: Guitar,
   piano. sax. mandolin
Hobbies: Fishing, records
Favourite colour: Blue
Favourite singers: Cliff Richard,
   Cilla Black, Sonny Boy
                      Williamson
Favourite actors and actresses:
   Audie Murphy, Raymond
   Massey, Betty Davis
Favourite food: English
Favourite drink: Milk
Favourite clothes: Casual
Favourite Composers: John
   Lennon, Paul McCartney
   Spector, Beethoven
Likes: Long hair on girls,
                      travelling
Dislikes   Marmite
Best friend: Mom
Tastes in music: Ballad, rave,
                      classical
Pets: Dog—"Taffy"
Personal ambition: Buy mom and
   dad a house
Professional ambition: Successful
                      musician
Favourite Groups: Beatles
   Shadows, Platters,
   Kinks, Stones

One of my first features in the
local press. I've never played the
sax in my life...

Picture courtesy of Chris Selby

The 'N Betweens' misspelled business contract.

No, not Abbey Road London but Wolverhampton!

Picture courtesy of Chris Selby

The 'N Betweens. Now just me, Don, Jim and Nod. On our way to becoming Slade.
Picture courtesy of Chris Selby

It was our publicist Keith Altham's idea for us to become skinheads.
Picture courtesy of Chris Selby

Chas Chandler. Our manager and much, much more than that.

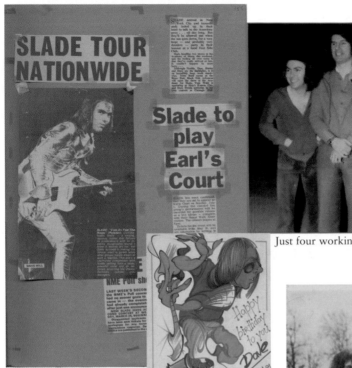

SLADE TOUR NATIONWIDE

Slade to play Earl's Court

NME POLL

Happy Birthday to you Dave

Just four working class lads from the Black Country.

Fans send me scrapbooks, photos, mementos, all sorts of treasures.

SLADE FAN CLUB NEWS

13 SOUTH MOLTON STREET, LONDON, W.1

Hello!
All together now, to the tune of "Twenty-One Today" — "Number One Again, Number One Again!!". That's the triumphant song echoing round our offices at the moment. As you probably realise, my news has to be sent off to Superstar some time before you read it in the mag., owing to the date everything has to be ready for the printers. But even if the chart scene is slightly different by now, there's no changing the fact that Slade have clocked up another solid gold smash! It's the first time a record has been released and leapt straight into the No. 1 slot since the Beatles did it in 1969.
Any of you who managed a trip to Wembley to see our lads on the 29th of March will have noticed something new. For those who didn't manage to get there, I'll let you out of your suspense long enough to tell you that Slade have changed their stage gear. Wait till we get our latest set of photos developed and you'll be able to see what we mean! All the new clothes have been designed by—guess who!—that talented lad Dave Hill himself, while his dedicated Mum was kind enough to do all sewing. (Thanks, Mum!)
Slade's European tour, which was broken to allow them to fly back from Yugoslavia for the Wembley concerts (originally there was only one planned, but so many people wanted tickets that they arranged an extra one!) continues right up until the end of April. After that there are rumours in the air of another American tour, but nothing has yet been finalised. Slade's manager, Chas Chandler, is over there at the moment, keeping an eye on the U.S. record charts! The next English tour may be in May. If any English tour dates are confirmed in the meantime, you'll find them published in the 'On The Road' spot of MICKIE Message & Songbook.
Lots of you have written to me asking if Nod has found himself a house yet. Well, Don has bought a huge old white Bentley, but Nod says that's not big enough for him to live in and he's waiting for Buckingham Palace to be put up for sale! Talking about Nod, when the group had their celebration last month after receiving all the awards they'd won last year, you should have seen the 'knees up' that he did. He won a great round of applause from everyone after his strenuous leaping exhibition! All good training for his on-stage efforts, of course.
Hope you all saw the group on Crackerjack, by the way. Did you know that they had also appeared on French television, as a kind of musical break during the televising of the French elections. They're all very proud 'cos it was a great honour for them to be chosen.
Whew! Run out of space again. I'll be back next month, so keep on stomping till then.
Luv,
DIANA

Slade, chart toppers and award-winners. On a boat, on the Thames, and on the 'pop'...

We have the best fans in the world and had an incredibly popular and well run fan club.

1977, Cologne. Pre-gig tuning with Jim.

Swin, our roadie, and Don's mate from school.

Don, Leandra, Nod's first wife, Nod and Jan and me, at the promotor Mel Bush's wedding reception in 1982.

My wedding car business. The Roller with my Jensen.

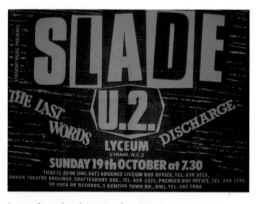

I wonder what happened to U2...

The house in Solihull. Oddly enough right next to a girls' school...
© *Sunday Mirror*

That round bath cost a fortune.
© *Sunday Mirror*

In the back garden
at Solihull. Jan was
pregnant with Jade at
the time.

At Solihull, in a reflective mood!

Lord and Lady Hill, of
Solihull...

Carol, Dad and me in Wolverhampton in the late 1960s.

Me and Jan, living it up, in one of the posh Solihull restaurants.

On holiday, with my gorgeous Jan, in the early 1970s.

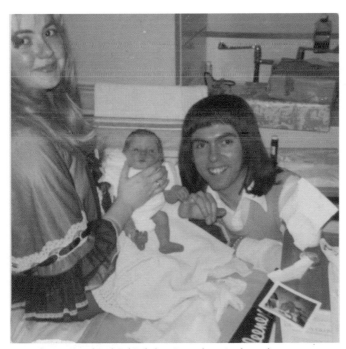

I may have missed Jade's birth but I got there in the end.

In the Falklands, not that long after the war had ended.

In Russia with Don and Trevor Holliday and our bodyguards...

Me and Don. Fifty years on, we're still the best of mates and still having fun.

At the Life After Stroke Awards London, 2016. I do my best to support this charity which means so much to me.

With the extended family, after receiving my honorary degree from the University of Wolverhampton.
© *University of Wolverhampton*

Me and Len Tuckey. He was instrumental in getting Slade back on the road.
© *Rudi Breitneicher*

Abbie Carter. Simply the linchpin for me and Slade.

Slade alive today! John, Don, me and Mal.

My family. My everything.
© *Graham Stroud*

Who'd have thought. Fifty years with Slade, and in my seventies, that I'd still be rockin' the world!

that had a recording of someone shouting 'Attention – House Being Robbed!' So I went into the house and was met by a smell of cigarettes, and there was this note. It was from some fans and they wanted to apologise for breaking into my house. They didn't nick anything – we had nothing to pinch! The note said, 'We're very sorry that we got inside your house. We knocked on the door but we wanted to get inside and we are really surprised because we don't really like your house. We thought you would live in a silver one. We thought you'd have something really super modern, we weren't expecting to come into a house with fuddy-duddy wallpaper!'

I was about to ring the police when the phone went and this little voice said, 'We're really sorry. Don't call the police. We didn't mean to do any harm, or any damage. We got in through a quarter-light. We'll pay for it.' They were only young girls, there may have been several of them. They said they were really, really sorry, so I didn't call the police maybe because of that time I'd broken into a school as a kid, not meaning any harm. And I was a bit relieved that it wasn't burglars. The other thing was that this was a time when nobody knew I was married, so they probably thought there was only me there, and somehow that made it feel better.

Later that day I went down the garden. There was a part like an orchard and a tree house there. I wasn't looking for anything in particular, but I must have noticed something so I went up to the tree house and there was a picture of Donny Osmond inside. It looked like they had spent the night there. I thought it was really funny that they had broken into my house and left a picture of Donny Osmond. 'We've broken into your house, mate, but we're into the Osmonds!'

We had no furniture until after we got married and Jan moved in properly. At first she found it magical, as you do when you get your first house together, but Solihull was a big adjustment for her too, going from a council house near Walsall into this huge place. After we had our first daughter, Jade, in 1975, I know it put a strain on her when I was away touring a lot. She was an hour away from her parents and a bit isolated. She'd tell me she was hoovering the house and she'd just burst into tears.

I wonder now if, as well as isolating us from our families, the house started to isolate me from the group a little bit too, because the other three still had places in the Wolverhampton and Walsall area. They used to moan when we were coming back up north and they had to come off the motorway and drive for miles to drop me home, because there was no M42 back then. They hated that!

Saying all of that, we had some great times in Solihull, and after we left there were times when we wished we'd stayed – although not now; we're very happy where we are. They were crazy times, we did some daft things, and we certainly spent some money on that house. One of my extravagant ideas was getting this really fancy round orange bath. Nobody had round baths, and it took for ever to fill! There were motifs around the side like fleurs-de-lis. The bathroom was all a bit Hollywood: we had thick white carpets, we had the shower done, then we had an artist who was a bathroom designer and he did two or three paintings. We spent a fortune on this ruddy bathroom.

But of course having it wasn't enough – I wanted to show it off – so we ended up using this bath in a German magazine feature, which Chas set up. This German guy, Booby, wanted to do a feature on where we all lived, so he came round the house. Jan was at work at the hairdresser's at the time, so I was in on my own. Booby had organised this motorbike, a Benelli, for the photo session. It was a big bike and I really couldn't ride it. They also turned up with a Japanese girl. I didn't know why she was there, but they knew I had this round bath so suddenly it's, 'Do you mind if we have a picture of you and this girl in your bath?' Not only that, but she was going to strip off. 'It'll look amazing.'

I didn't think Jan would be of quite the same opinion, so I called her at work and it was, 'No way! I'm coming home!' In the end we finished up doing the shoot with me and Jan in the bath, drinking champagne. It was a showy sort of, 'We're doing good here. Cheers!' There was a lot of that going on, and I was rolling with it. It was just what a pop star did. Those pictures ended up in the *Daily Mirror*, and the bath makers, Bonsack, contacted me, thanking me for the plug!

We weren't doing things by halves at that stage. I decided we should get a dog to go with this big new house, so I got a big dog, a Great Dane. Well, he wasn't big when we got him. I got him to look after Jan when I was away for six weeks. When I came back, he was huge, eating the house! The dog was named Windsor. The band were sitting in a car one day and I said I was trying to think of a name for the dog. Suspension Bridge came up, stupid names. I said I needed something a bit more stately, so Nod came up with Windsor, 'That sounds a bit royal, doesn't it?' he said.

At first Windsor lived in the house, but then we had to have a kennel built for him outside. He was good at escaping was Windsor. One time, my sister Carol came to look after the house when Jan came over to America with me and the police brought the dog home. He'd got out of the garden and had gone for a walk around Beatties, the department store in Solihull. It was like having a small horse in the shop and those dogs slobber a lot!

The next time he got out was worse. Carol was housesitting again, and he got into the neighbour's. The lady next door, very posh, was on her lawn having tea and crumpets with her husband, and Windsor dropped a massive turd right in front of her. The old boy went nuts. He came round and banged on the door. 'This damn dog has just been on the lawn and done a bloody great number. It has really upset my wife who has had to go indoors!' Eventually the dog went to Dad because Jan was pregnant and we were worried about such a big dog with a baby at home. Dad didn't want me to have it put into a home, and that was wonderful because I know he had some nice years with the dog.

We only had the one party there, I think, although I didn't really want it. I was a proper house owner by then and had visions of cigarette burns in the carpet. Anyway, at two o'clock in the morning, knock, knock, knock, the next-door neighbour was back at the door, this time in his pyjamas. 'I can't sleep because of the terrible noise. Can you turn the music down?' Despite being the very image of drugged-up pop stars we apologised and promised to turn it down. He was invited in by someone, probably one of the band. It wasn't the most raucous party, but we probably had the French windows open at the back.

That was how it was at the time. We couldn't stop selling records and tickets and were as close as anybody to becoming the new Beatles. All we had to do now was make a movie and conquer America…

13

SLADE IN FLAME

Success, especially the kind we enjoyed in 1973, can be a double-edged sword. When you're at the very top like we were, a band with six UK number ones and nine top-four singles in the previous couple of years, how do you top that? The answer is that you can't, especially in the music business, which is all about change and new fashions and styles coming up all the time. What you have to do is maintain what you've got, but you also need to find new things to do, to diversify if you like, and get bigger and better that way.

Being as big as we were was great not just because of the fame and the success, but because it meant new opportunities were coming all the while. One of these was making a film. In some ways, it was the obvious thing to do – those were the days when it was another thing you did if you were in a hit group. We weren't entirely sold on it because we weren't sure what kind of a story we wanted and we certainly weren't actors. Chas was very big on it though, partly because I think he saw it as opening up

America, and that was our other preoccupation of the time, getting hits over there.

The film idea caught us at what was an interesting time, because we were going through some changes as people and as musicians. If you listen to 'Everyday', which was our next single after the Christmas song, it had a more wistful, rueful feel to it. It caught the way we were thinking, even if we didn't necessarily realise it yet. Being away on the road all the time had been tough, and we were getting older. We were getting married or had long-term girlfriends, buying houses, settling down a bit. We didn't see the band as a grind, far from it, but maybe we were getting a bit world-weary.

Perhaps that played into what became the subject matter for the film. There'd been talk of it being a sci-fi thing – probably because of my silver costumes – but we didn't go for that. Then there was the question of acting. None of us had done any of that, so we didn't want to be doing anything that required too much from us – plus Don wouldn't be able to remember his lines that well because of the accident. In the end we settled on the obvious idea of the film being about a rock band, and this writer Andrew Birkin came on the road with us in America for a while to get a feel for what we were like, the way we behaved, so that he could write around that. That was a bit like how the Beatles had set up *A Hard Day's Night*, but we didn't want to copy that, so the idea evolved into us playing a fictitious band, Flame, from the 1960s, with bits of our story in there along with other stories from the pop business, creating this bigger tale. A lot of the ideas came about from us just talking about the past while we were in hotel rooms or travelling to gigs in the States.

Andrew, Jane Birkin's brother, was really good. He sat with each of us and got those stories about being in a group, like the one about one manager selling a band on to another. They used that in the film, and as I've already said, that was real life – we'd been through that.

It was an interesting process making a film, and we met some great characters as a result. Johnny Shannon, who'd been in *Performance*, was the dodgy geezer. He was involved in boxing away from acting and had some great stories to tell. Then there was Alan Lake, who was a great bloke but a tough guy as well. You didn't mess with him – any sign of trouble and he was taking his jacket off! He clearly had a drink problem and nearly lost his part in the film because of it. His was the classic case of being two different people, one when he was sober and the other when he'd had a couple. He got drunk and was involved in a bit of a scrap right at the start of filming and was going to get thrown off until his wife, Diana Dors, stepped in. She was his manager as well, I think.

We got invited down to their house in Sunningdale, which was great because Diana was a big star. It was a nice area, a leafy suburb, really posh. We drove down in my gold Rolls-Royce, pulled up and Diana came to the door. Then Alan comes out, and once he sees my car he thinks that his is a load of junk – he's only got a white Roller! On set we'd got used to Alan doing all the talking, but he wasn't like that when he was with Diana. He was very quiet. She was lovely, really nice, talking about playing the Northern clubs. She knew her stuff and talked sense. No trying to put on the glamour Hollywood style. Even so, she was a film star and took us into one room with a pool table where there were loads of pictures of her on the walls, really great pictures from the 1950s, and she looked amazing. And all the while Alan hardly spoke; Diana was totally in command of the conversation. Alan portrayed the singer Jack Daniels at the start of the film, and he could certainly sing. He was an actor but he knew what to do. He acted Daniels like P. J. Proby.

The film captured the rough, seedy side of things, which we certainly knew about – there were some unscrupulous people in our past – and ended up being a much darker film than we had imagined, quite gritty, and perhaps because of that, it's aged pretty well and nowadays people see it as a bit of a classic – Mark Kermode called it 'the *Citizen Kane* of British pop movies', which isn't bad going! Our original idea was for a comedy, which better suited our image, and I wasn't that taken with it when it came out, but in hindsight maybe the darker side subconsciously reflected the period we were going into ourselves.

It was certainly the way films were tending to go at that point. *Flame* was overseen by David Puttnam, and he was involved in *That'll Be the Day* and *Stardust* with David Essex around the same time, so I'm sure that played into it as well. We weren't in control of what that film was going to be. We were recording, we were touring, we were new to film, it all got left in the hands of other people because making a film is a big production compared with making a record which only needed the four of us, an engineer and Chas really.

I do think *Flame* might have confused our fans because we were the band that you turned to when things weren't going well, we were the band that was all about enjoying yourself, the happy-go-lucky group. That was what all those singles in 1973 had been about. We were a good-time group, but this wasn't a feel-good film by any means, especially that lift sequence at the end where nobody in the band wants to know each other anymore.

In that sense, maybe doing that movie wasn't the best choice. *Flame* had gangsters, toes being chopped off, a really nasty edge to it. A director of *Top of the Pops* came to the premiere and said, 'Do you think you've done the right thing? Sometimes you're showing things that we're all trying to hide.' That hit the nail on the head.

I think people started wondering if that was what we were really like, and that wasn't helped by the fact that we spent a lot of time out of the country in 1974 and especially 1975, trying to break America, so people weren't seeing us, and before the Internet it was very much out of sight, out of mind. Then you'd got the songs on the soundtrack. I think they were some of our very best stuff, songs like 'How Does It Feel' and 'Far Far Away', but they were more reflective songs and we hadn't shown that side of us in the past, not as singles anyway. This was Slade in a lower key, not so in your face, not the party group any longer, though we were still very capable of being that, especially on stage.

The soundtrack album stands up as a good piece of work for me. 'So Far So Good' is a good song, and Nod wrote the lyrics as a take on where we were at that point. In the film we're sitting on the back of a spinning boat, and we're singing, 'So far so good, doing what we could, taking chances.' We were creating more depth in our music, maybe because of the way we'd had to record differently to accommodate Don. I also think Jim was starting to enjoy using the tools in the studio a lot more and he took every opportunity to experiment. We got some great stuff out of that, though Chas wasn't entirely happy with it. I remember when we did 'Wishing You Were Here' Chas thought it was namby-pamby, but I really liked it. We were making some good recordings through 1974 and having hits. Things were still really strong for us, but we were definitely changing, perhaps starting to pull in different directions too.

Music as a whole was going through another period of change because 1974 was the last hurrah for glam rock. Bowie had killed off Ziggy Stardust the year before and was moving on; a lot of artists like Mud, Sweet, Alvin Stardust, all the glam rock acts were having their final hits and the wheel was turning again, not that we knew that much about it because after *Flame* came out in early 1975, we really did turn our attention to America.

One vivid memory of the whole *Flame* experience was the run of film premieres, especially the one in Wolverhampton. Mom had never come to any of the gigs that I can remember – she was never well enough – though Dad would always be there, but she did come to the premiere in Wolverhampton. There was a photograph of her in the *Express & Star*, but she didn't look good. She went through a whole physical change when she became ill. Her features changed, and before she died I remember Dad saying to me, 'I looked at her one day and I could see straight through her,' like he was looking at a ghost. It was a warning. I think he was trying to say to me, 'She won't be here much longer.'

The end came in 1976. I remember I had a phone call. I was in Solihull, and Dad called and said, 'Your mom's died.' I can't remember crying or anything. I went over to Wolverhampton and Dad was sitting downstairs. He said, 'I didn't know till the morning.' He had gone to wake her up in the morning and she was freezing cold. She had died in the night. He asked if I wanted to go upstairs and see her but I couldn't face it.

Although she had only just died, I felt like she had gone a long time before. Jan says that I never mourned my mother's death and I don't think I have. Maybe I built up a resistance or an acceptance of the way that she was. I think I had come to accept that she would always be that way.

In the end I think it was simply a release for her.

14

TRYING TO CRACK AMERICA

In the early part of the 1970s, the fact that Slade were such a diverse group was one of our strengths in the UK, in Europe and Australia, places where we were absolutely huge. We could appeal to the pop fans with hits such as 'Coz I Luv You'; we had that reflective, ballad side to us with 'Everyday', and things like 'Far Far Away' or 'Cum On Feel The Noize' were anthems in different ways, and then on the albums and on stage we were a good, hard-rocking group as well. We'd got a lot of things cooking, and that was to our advantage because we reached out right across the spectrum of music fans.

But in America it was a different story. They liked to put music into pigeonholes, because that tended to be the way FM radio was organised over there – you had rock stations, blues stations, pop, country – you knew what you were going to get. The programmers never knew which one of those to put us in. Perhaps it was the sound of our records too, which were quite gritty at a time when

American music had a real sheen to it. Even Suzi Quatro, an American girl from Detroit who made it in Britain, had similar issues when she went back to the States – her records didn't quite sit right on the radio either.

Chas had always seen the Beatles as the blueprint for us, and so obviously America was the last great frontier for us to conquer, not least because that's where the mega-money was, which is what any manager is always looking for. We'd spent chunks of time out there in 1973 and 1974, but we were always dashing back across the Atlantic to play shows here and in Europe, to promote singles, to record and so on, so it wasn't our main focus. We were accused of not committing ourselves to it, and it was probably true that on a couple of occasions when we looked like we might break through, we'd headed home to do something else. So this time, after we'd played a tour of the UK in the spring of 1975, we decided, very much at Chas's urging, to effectively relocate to the States for what turned out to be around eighteen months to crack the market over there.

Before we went, we did a photo shoot wearing the Stars and Stripes. Some of the press started to call us Yankee Doodle Dandies, and that didn't go down well at home. People said we were selling out. The daft thing about that was you had all these big British rock groups who were exiles and living outside Britain because of the 90 per cent tax, but we came home every chance we got and never mind having to pay tax!

We decided to base ourselves in New York because that was one of the cities where we were at our strongest, the record company was there, and it was good for getting at the East Coast market and for travel across America generally. Obviously the move across the Atlantic was complicated by family considerations. To start with, we all stayed in an apartment block, an aparthotel, and then we each got proper apartments in decent parts of New York – and remember, New York in 1975 was a pretty rough place if you were in the wrong part. We had use of the record company limousines, and the limo drivers would say, 'I ain't going down there!' We'd ask to be taken to Harlem and get the reply, 'You've got to be joking! Don't roll the windows down, and if you need the toilet we ain't gonna stop!' It was all a bit scary. As English people, we weren't used to no-go areas. We had all grown up with cowboy films and shoot-outs, we knew Americans had guns, but this was for real.

It got very real at one point when Jan and Jade got caught up in a bank robbery while I was away doing a gig. Jan had taken Jade out in the buggy and gone into a bank, and suddenly there was a hold-up going on. There was this robber with a gun and he made them all lie on the floor. Jan had to tip the buggy backwards so Jade was upside down. The robber started waving his pistol around, shouting for everyone to be quiet. Eventually the cops turned up and were firing bullets all over the place. One lady tried to help Jan and Jade and accidently got shot in the shoulder. The police eventually shot the robber, who it turned out had only a dummy gun.

Of course there were no mobile phones then, so we didn't know anything about this until we got back from the gig. Fortunately, Peter Kauff, who was a radio producer at the King Biscuit Flower Hour and involved with us in the States, had stayed in New York and he was able to look after them until we got back. He went out for dinner with Jim's wife, Louise, and Leandra, Nod's girlfriend, and calmed them down, they were all pretty shook up, it was a pretty frightening thing.

In spite of things like that, it was an interesting experience to live in another country, another culture, but it was a real adjustment to make, especially when we were living in the aparthotel because we never quite felt at home. The other complication for me and Jan was that we had Jade. That meant getting babysitters and the like, and early on we had this dumpy woman who used to eat everything out of the fridge. She would come in and scoff everything. Jade didn't like her and screamed at her every time she turned up. Then we had a more elderly lady, much calmer, called Monica, and Jade was OK with her, but obviously those things were always on Jan's mind especially as we tried to settle in.

Getting our own place did help, although that was a saga too because a lot of people wouldn't let us their apartments because we had a child. I walked into some apartments, pushing Jade's buggy, and got the cold shoulder. New Yorkers didn't know me, Slade weren't famous in America, I was just another prospective tenant. In the end we sorted it, but it was a reminder for me of a world where your face didn't get you anywhere. It was nice to be anonymous at times after the madness in England but I did miss the advantages that came with being famous!

Relocating over there made sense because, for all the success we'd had elsewhere, we hadn't had anything approaching that in the States. 'Gudbuy T'Jane' was the biggest hit we'd had, and that had only reached number sixty-eight. We weren't in a position of strength as far as the American market was concerned, but we were certainly going to make a huge effort to get them to sit up and take notice. In retrospect, that was actually part of our undoing because the record company were pushing us as the next Beatles. The hype was huge, and I remember one of the journalists saying, 'You guys had better be able to walk on water the way they're pushing you.' It's not easy doing that in platform boots.

I think that approach got the Americans' backs up, especially as we hadn't had a hit there yet. They took it as the company saying the States must be stupid not to have caught on to us like the rest of the world. But as we found out, America doesn't have much interest in what the rest of the world thinks or does. It likes to make up its own mind. They wanted to discover us, not have us forced down their throats.

There's an old saying that America and England are two countries divided by a common language, and that was true. We should have seen that problem coming because they'd put subtitles on *Flame*, so they were obviously having trouble with our accents. But other things didn't translate either. In Britain and Europe, no matter what Nod said on stage, everything was great, you'd get a reaction. Then we went to America, and most people didn't know us but, more important, they couldn't understand us either, musically or as people, and I don't think we ever fully worked out what to do about that.

We had a taste of that when we filmed a big TV show called *Midnight Special*, which went out across the country late at night, a cross between the *Old Grey Whistle Test* and Jools Holland's *Later* show. From the off it wasn't right. We were on with a lot of other artists who were successful in the States – the Guess Who, Leo Kottke, Judi Pulver – very laid back, like it was still Woodstock. When we followed them with all the glitz and the platform shoes, people must have thought, *What the hell is that?* All the record company were there expecting to celebrate, but it just didn't go well. There were technical problems on top of everything else, and I remember all of us feeling quite down about it on the night. Chas came in with, 'Don't worry, lads, there's much more to be done,' but the press reaction wasn't at all favourable. Maybe we were too full-on for them.

Technical problems were a regular feature in America. We took our PA with us, which was stupid because American PAs were really happening. Ours wasn't in the same class as American gear, but unfortunately we didn't know any better and just didn't think of hiring local equipment. Even our amplifiers were exported and because of their power change, from 240 to 110, although we had a voltage changer, it really upsets the amps. It wasn't the same sound as we had in England, which was awesome. We used Hi-Watt amplifiers, the same as the Who, but in America they lost something, and voltage converters would not rectify it. We just couldn't feel that power, which meant we didn't grab the audience the way we did in Britain. The sound fell out of the amps, it didn't fly out.

On top of that, a lot of the gigs we played were as support, which brings its own challenges for all kinds of reasons, but one of them was that suddenly we were in arenas and stadiums, not clubs and theatres, which was where we felt at home. We liked being physically close on stage, we were supportive of each other, we sparked off each other. Now Jim was half a mile away from me on the other side of the stage. The sound was split too, so where previously everything was pushed together and we were hearing each other as a unit, suddenly it was separated, and for a while that was off-putting.

When you're playing rock music in the way we'd done everywhere else, you harness the power and it gives you a sense of confidence, hearing that big sound. So at a point when we were a bit vulnerable anyway, hearing just yourself coming out of a monitor was disorientating. It took time to learn how to make that work for us, and until we did we probably played less as a band and more as individuals because that's what we were hearing. That lost the great strength of Slade, the sum of the parts being greater than the individuals, and that began to put a strain on the unity that we had, particularly as we couldn't make the headway we wanted to out there.

Looking back, we probably didn't appreciate just how different the States is to the rest of the world. I don't think we really understood the market we were trying to tap into, and Chas wasn't always around to help out either. He also had other things he was interested in, and we couldn't turn to him for advice or support in the way we had been able to back home.

Perhaps if Chas had been with us more, things might have worked out better in the States, but forty years on, I know for sure we were the right act, with the right songs, but maybe we were just in the wrong place at the wrong time. I remember talking to some of the guys from Status Quo around the same time, and they'd just come to the conclusion that America wasn't for them and were going to concentrate on the rest of the world, where it was happening for them, and keep things going back home. Maybe they made the right choice.

In America the musical mood was certainly very different to how it was in Britain. They were very much in that singer-songwriter era, that Laurel Canyon, California rock thing with James Taylor, Joni Mitchell, the Eagles. It was very smooth, late-night music and sounded great on FM radio – stuff like 'Hotel California', 'Sweet Home Alabama', the Doobie Brothers, Steely Dan. We felt generally out of place in America, especially in LA. People were laid-back, but we were nothing like that. And there were the Grateful Dead of course, who we played with at a festival in Philadelphia. You got stoned on the atmosphere of the place, there was so much dope in the air. We'd go to places and the audience would be sitting cross-legged on the floor, getting stoned, because America was very much into album rock at the time. Singles were unfashionable.

One of the ironies of the time was that we ended up supporting Kiss a few times. They were on the way to being huge, partly as a result of a live record called *Alive!* That sounded familiar! They were big fans of ours and were always very open about their influences: 'We don't forget Slade.' They'd obviously watched and listened to us, and that was true of a lot of bands. We were a band's band over there rather than a critic's band, and in America you need good press because of the size of the country.

In certain parts of America we did do good business, but we couldn't get arrested in others. But that happens even to American bands – the new wave stuff from 1976, Television, Patti Smith, Talking Heads, only really worked on the East Coast. For us, the hit that would really push us forward always seemed to be elusive. I remember running into Kim Fowley again after one of our gigs and he said, 'You were really good. But you didn't take the rough edges off it, did you?' Maybe we needed to become more American to succeed there, the way Rod Stewart or Led Zeppelin did. But that was alien to us, we were still four Black Country lads.

We were fish out of water at times. Everything about America is larger than anywhere else. If you go to a steakhouse, the steaks are bigger, there is more choice. Wherever we went, it took ages to order a meal because of all the things on the menu which they ask if you want in addition. You go through a whole roster of combinations until you get to the main course. The one time, we said we liked Indian food, and they thought we wanted to go to an American Indian restaurant and thought we were cool until we said we meant a curry house.

When things aren't going well, everybody thrashes around looking for reasons, and at times it did get silly. One time Chas told me I had to stop wearing platform boots. 'They associate them with drugs. If you don't stop wearing them, I'll pull my money out.' Faced with that, I didn't wear the boots that night. I got some trainers and actually felt pretty good – it was much easier to move around. But then you look at Kiss and there was Gene Simmons with platforms two or three times bigger than anything I ever had. Didn't do them any harm!

It was turning a bit sour at that point, and Chas was having a lot of arguments with the people we were working with over there, who didn't agree with his ideas and the way he was trying to direct things. There were some blazing rows between him and Peter Kauff. The longer it went on without us getting that breakthrough, the more money was being spent. We were staying in good hotels, so good that when we went into some of them, we wouldn't put our bags down because we couldn't afford to give the bellboy a tip for carrying them. Chas was spending a lot of money on us in America at this point without too much return, and it was getting to him. Certainly money was being spent and no expense spared. We were checked into the Hyatt House on Sunset Boulevard, they'd got a swimming pool on the top floor. When we arrived at the hotel, there was a big sign, 'Welcome Slade!' There were a couple of notorious groupies outside because obviously we were the next band in – they'd obviously been welcoming everyone else before!

We arrived there in the regular record company car – we put the road manager and the crew in the limos that had been sent to the airport for us, so everybody thought we were ultra-cool because we weren't travelling in limousines. LA was certainly colourful. It didn't look so great in daylight, that's what I noticed. It looked like a lot of sheds! But at night, it was wonderful, surreal.

In LA we stayed at the Hyatt House and the Beverly Wilshire, top hotels, because he always wanted to impress the Americans, but we were the sort of people who would have been down the local Frankie and Benny's and been quite happy.

We hadn't got a record that sounded right on American radio, so we decided that making our next album there might be a way to solve that problem. We checked back into the Record Plant in New York where we'd done the Christmas song and started to put together what became *Nobody's Fools*. It took quite a while to do, because we were determined not to rush anything, so we had six weeks of working on it. We were really pleased with it when it was done, but again it barely dented the American market, and on top of that the album only got to number fourteen when we put it out in the UK, which made it pretty clear that by being away for so long, people had left us behind and moved on to other groups.

That was when the doubts started to set in within the group, and we began to lose our focus and, on occasion, our professionalism. It was hard to go from top of the pile at home to bottom of the bill in America and to see no light at the end of the tunnel, and without Chas there all the time, we had nobody to keep us in check. Chas finally caught up with us at a club gig. We could see him out in the audience, watching us with this look on his face like, *My God! What's happened to them?* Afterwards he came and saw us in the dressing room. 'I should have kept an eye on you – you're going down the nick. There are people walking out!'

So Nod said to him, 'There were more who walked out last night,' like tonight had been a success, and Chas went mad. 'Noddy, is that how you judge your shows? By the number who walk out?' We had gone down the pan because we had lost our impetus. We couldn't see the way ahead; we couldn't see how it was going to work; we were demoralised. America can do that to you.

People at home kept saying, 'When are you going to crack America?' but the truth was, it was cracking us. It had been a catalogue of mistakes and we were getting tired of it. We wanted to get back to what we knew. Plain and simple, we'd had enough. So the band asked me to phone Chas and tell him we wanted to come home – it always seemed to be me that did those things, just like in the early days when I had to go to the door of the B & B where we wanted to stay and charm the landlady! And he said to me, 'Oh, you want to throw the towel in, do you?' He argued that we were close to a breakthrough but in truth we weren't close at all, nowhere near. If anything, we were getting further away.

In 'Far Far Away' Nod had written the lyric, 'The call of home is loud,' and for us that was true. At the start of August 1976, it was time to go home.

15

THE READING FESTIVAL AND REBIRTH

When we got back to England, it was to find that things had changed a lot musically while we'd been away. We'd done OK in the charts: 'In For A Penny' and 'Let's Call It Quits' both made it to number eleven either side of Christmas 1975 and both had hung around for a while, so that was reasonably encouraging considering we hadn't been around to promote them. But looking at the chart in August '76, it was very different, even if Elton was number one with Kiki Dee. Disco was starting to get a hold on things, while on the live scene something called punk rock was getting kids excited.

They were uncertain times for us. We took the rest of 1976 to get a new album together and released that in March '77 ahead of tours in Scandinavia, the UK and Germany, all good territories for us. If *Nobody's Fools* had an American slant to it, this one was a lot more focused on the Slade sound of old. It was a good rock record and one that has had a lot of fans down the years – years later Nirvana said it was an influence on them.

It wasn't on Polydor this time, but on Barn, Chas's own label. He picked the title as well, from some graffiti he'd seen somewhere. *Whatever Happened To Slade?* was meant to be tongue-in-cheek now that we were back in the UK, but a lot of critics took it at face value – the few critics who reviewed it anyway because by now the music press was all about other, newer bands. We were seen as old hat, and that was frustrating because we thought we'd made a good record and we were a better live band than we'd ever been. But if you can't get publicity, it becomes very hard to get your message out to the public, and without a big record company spending money on us either, it was a struggle. The tickets didn't sell for the UK tour the way they had before, the single 'Gypsy Roadhog' only reached number forty-eight, and the album didn't chart at all. It was America all over again, only this time at home.

For a while we were just thrashing around, not knowing what to do. We tried all sorts of things. I shaved all my hair off, got a leather jacket and Doc Martens and tried to give us a harder image to blend in with the times, but that didn't do anything. I suppose that was symptomatic of where we were then, how far out of the loop we were after being in America so long. In the hits years Chas said that I was always 'next year, this year', meaning I got there first with the image and the clothes. But now I was copying things, trying to catch up with the scene – we all were. We released a string of non-album singles to try and spark something off, but nothing took off, even though we tried the serious stuff and we tried the daft stuff, because both have always been valid parts of what Slade is about.

Nod was very much on my side with this kind of thinking, although Jim was more attracted by the serious musician side of it all, the more so the longer we spent in recording studios. But let's face it, we were the only serious band that could have put 'Okey Cokey' out as a single! That was a reflection of just how lost we were at that time, but because we'd get the audience jumping round to it at gigs, we recorded it. The record pluggers were totally embarrassed to take it to the Radio 1 playlist, but it was a really funny record. Of course, it didn't do anything.

Having at least played town and city halls and the like in 1977, a year later we were back playing the clubs in a lot of smaller towns, and when you are down like that, everyone is stressed out, and I felt that I was something of a scapegoat for a while. This was early in '78, after a couple more singles had failed. I was called to a meeting with the others and told that I was on the carpet, that I wasn't pulling my weight and nor was Don.

Certainly there were money issues at the time. We'd stopped selling records, and the tours weren't doing so well. Meanwhile Chas had other issues to deal with. He was getting divorced and was setting up Barn, his record label, and ultimately it became clear that he'd spent publishing royalties due to Jim and Nod. That eventually led to him giving Jim and Nod his share of the catalogue to pay off the debt. With all that going on in the background and with us getting nowhere in the charts, people were starting to get desperate and having to do things they didn't want. I ended up selling the house in Solihull for instance, as I'll come back to later.

Everybody was trying to find a way back to the top, and I suspected somebody was thinking about the possibility of finding new musicians for Jim and Nod to work with, so as to try and change course and re-energise Slade. The odd thing about that was I had never really had much songwriting input anyway, so if our new songs weren't popular, it wasn't down to my writing. Nobody was thinking that clearly, and turning the money side around was all the more pressing now because we had families, houses and other commitments.

Just how serious they were about getting rid of me and Don I don't know because suddenly Chas got a call with an offer of a few weeks playing in Poland – some big shows, outdoors too, good money, and so all those conversations just disappeared overnight and we were on our way there, all forgotten. It was all very weird, but it did leave a bit of a sour taste. The idea that I might have to leave the group that I'd formed was tough to take and preyed on my mind for quite a while. It was unsettling, but at the same time the Poland thing coming up was comforting. We'd always said, right back to the earliest days, that if we were struggling, something would turn up. Poland was some kind of evidence that it would.

Saying that, when we got back from there things were still really tough in the UK. We worked really hard, we played anywhere that would have us – clubs, universities, colleges, Meccas, even the chicken-in-a-basket places we swore we'd never do – but there didn't seem to be any glimmer of hope back home. We'd do places and look at who was on the week after, and it would be bands like XTC or the Cure, groups who you hadn't really heard of at the time. But they were playing these places on the way up, and that was pretty sobering. We were doing anything that we could to earn some money from live work because the record royalties weren't there, and for Don and I especially they were really hard times. But we did it to keep the band together in the belief that something would turn up. We felt we were still playing well, we were a good rock band, we still had lots to offer.

But you can hold on to a dream only so long before reality overwhelms you, and I reached that point in 1980. We'd put out an EP, *Six of the Best*. It had some strong material on it, but again there was no reaction. It didn't make the charts, and I started to wonder if I needed to get out and do something else. I was pretty disillusioned.

I'd still got the gold Rolls-Royce, so I had this idea that I was going to go into the wedding car business, kind of 'rent a pop star for the big day', driving the bride to the church in the Roller. That was where I was, financially and mentally. I was ready to give that a go, pack the band in, when I got a call from Chas: 'Listen, Davy, we've got a slot at the Reading Festival. Ozzy Osbourne can't get his group together in time, and they're offering us his spot.' The Reading Festival was a big deal, three days over the

August bank holiday weekend, but I was so disillusioned with it all, I didn't want to go on.

Nod got on to me then, trying to persuade me, but I wasn't interested. 'They're all heavy metal bands, and we're from the seventies – they won't like us.' UFO were on the bill. Def Leppard were just making a name for themselves. Whitesnake were on and Budgie. But they chipped away at me. Chas got on to me about this fantastic opportunity for a great live band like us, and they talked me round. I didn't want to let the others down, so I thought, *Let's see what we can do. I can do the wedding business afterwards.* It turned out that it was one of those sliding doors moments in life.

It was a nice sunny day, and I remember driving there through Oxford. All these groups were turning up in Rolls-Royces, but we went in the wrong entrance and parked in the punters' car park. We weren't even advertised, but the fella on the gate recognised us and let us in. The first person we saw inside was Tommy Vance, the Radio 1 DJ who did the *Friday Rock Show*, who was doing all the announcements at the festival. We went to our caravan and Tommy said, 'I think you are going to do really well today.' He said something about it being boring and all the bands posing, trying to be something they weren't. That was promising, but I can't deny that we were really nervous as we went on stage – I certainly was.

But everything just seemed to click. We played three songs straight off – didn't give anyone a chance to say, 'We like you,' or, 'We hate you.' In terms of playing, we were in great nick. We were really good at this point because we had done all the universities, we were gigging regularly, we were ready. Nod's voice was also really cock on – he sounded great. We played a lot faster than our records. They were a good tempo anyway, but with the years and years of live gigs, we were really at the top of our game and we knocked the crowd sideways – 40,000 people. These were kids who had grown up listening to us and were now off at college or in jobs, hearing and enjoying us again.

Our second song was 'Take Me Bak 'Ome'. It was going down great, and that started us looking at each other on stage. By the time we finished the third song, we could tell it was OK and we were flying. Our stage act was well structured, hitting the crowd with a load of hits at the end, but the bit that got us was when they all started to shout 'Merry Christmas!' Nod is a great frontman and knows what to say. He lured them in, then said, 'No, I'm not going to do it – you do it!' So we're standing there not doing anything, and they're singing the Christmas song at us in the middle of the summer! It was weird. We had never experienced that. We had only ever done that song at Christmas.

Chas was like a Cheshire cat, standing at the side of the stage, looking at me. I was pleased that he was pleased. I came off and there were no phone boxes on site, which was annoying because I wanted to tell Jan what had happened. We couldn't believe it. We were so elated. It was like the Lincoln Festival all over again. If we hadn't done that show, I'm sure I would have left, and probably we would have all called it quits, but it gave us a second chance.

We put out a live EP from Reading – Radio 1 had recorded the whole festival – and though it wasn't a massive hit, it did get us back in the charts. It stuck around for five weeks, and that edged us back into the mainstream, albeit in a slightly different way. Now we were a live band again rather than a singles act, back to our roots. Either side of Christmas 1980, we played a big tour in the UK, getting back to the venues we'd seen in 1972–73, the likes of the Hammersmith Odeon, Birmingham Odeon, Liverpool Empire, Manchester Apollo.

In early 1981 we released 'We'll Bring The House Down', which got up to number ten and was in the singles chart for a couple of months, and suddenly we were really back. It was different to how it had been – there wasn't the hysteria of the early seventies – but we were doing good business. We were getting respect and we'd earned ourselves another crack at success.

16

RUNAWAY SUCCESS

That second burst of success was very welcome, especially financially, but 1980s Slade was never going to be the same as seventies Slade. The business had changed, but there was more to it than that. We weren't the same people that we'd been ten years before. We'd been through a lot, grown up a bit and found that when you get to your thirties the world is different to how it was when you were chasing your first dreams.

Certainly we wanted to make the best of this second chance, but there were other things competing for our time now, in terms of family in particular. As you get older, you can't ever get back to the 'Four Musketeers' thing you have when you're young and making your way. Back in the 1970s it was the band that came first, second and third, we had that unity, that single-minded drive, that common purpose, regardless of what we were like individually, what our tastes were like and what our girlfriends were like. The four of us would come together to do what we did, and there was never any 'I can't make it because my girlfriend wants me to go out somewhere' with Jim, me, Don or Nod. We were never unreliable in that way. There was this loyalty to the group, although in hindsight that gave rise to decisions that I'm not proud of.

I wasn't there in 1975 when Jan gave birth to Jade, our first child, and I wasn't there because I decided to do a television show we had booked in Holland. Jan hadn't had the baby, she was at home, she was pregnant and very close, and then she went into hospital just as I left to do this telly thing. It was not wanting to let the band down, and I must admit I didn't think my decision was the right one even then. But would I do it again? In honesty maybe I would, I can't rule it out. None of us wanted to be the one causing a problem. I was the first member of Slade to have a child, so it hadn't happened to the group before. None of us understood what it meant, so I just ploughed on. The band always came first, 'This is what men do – we earn the money We're this band of brothers.'

Second time around it was different. In early 1981 both Jan and Louise, Jim's wife, were pregnant. Our Sam was born in the spring, within a couple of weeks of Jim's son, and we were both much more present than I had been with Jade. I regret Jade not seeing as much of me as the other two kids did when they were young because I was off trying to bring some money in. Probably most blokes in their twenties and early thirties are doing that kind of thing, but my job meant me never being in one place for any time at all. I was always on the road – I didn't come home from the office at night. But by now we'd pretty much turned our backs on America, and the tours were in the UK, Germany, Sweden and Norway, so it was more manageable.

There were still ups and downs. We parted company with Chas in 1981, though he did help us negotiate a deal with RCA before that, a deal structured for the four of us which gave Don and me what we felt was a fairer share. The first real fruit of this was 'Lock Up Your Daughters', which was a top-thirty single, and we released an album around the same time, *Til Deaf Us Do Part*, which both carried on the tradition of jokey-sounding titles and also kept us tied in with our new heavy metal following post-Reading, something we'd fostered by playing the Monsters of Rock festival in '81 with AC/DC and Whitesnake.

I had a song on that album, 'M'Hat, M'Coat', the only solo tune I got onto a Slade album with the original four. The simplest way of putting it is that I lacked confidence in that department. I always felt my role in Slade was to be the guitar player with the distinctive sound, and then the one who got us in the papers with the costumes, the image. 'You write 'em, I'll sell 'em,' as I've mentioned already. And then when Jim and Nod emerged as this great songwriting team, how was I going to beat that? Nod described my song as being 'about Dave's guru'. That was something going on with me at the time – I was trying to find some meaning in life away from the band and the music.

I don't think I wanted to upset the balance in the band by pushing my songs. I remember around that stage I submitted four songs which Nod sang to the record company – he was very supportive – but the reaction was very iffy. They didn't like them, or 'We may do one.' I didn't say anything, just backed off, though I was a bit narked because a couple of them were really good, songs which I used later.

We consolidated things in 1982 with strong British tours at either end of the year, and Jan had our third child that autumn when Bibi was born. We were off the road for much of '83, putting together new material and doing outside projects, but all that was put on hold when we recorded 'My Oh My', which straight away everyone thought had real potential as a hit. We all put a lot into that. It was a great demo from Nod and Jim to start with, and we were all playing really well. I was very pleased with my solo on it – you could feel my excitement on the record – and the song was set to be a bit of an anthem.

RCA believed we would have a big hit with it and wanted it out in late November '83 because they saw it as a Christmas number one, ten years on from 'Merry Xmas Everybody'. We did *Top of the Pops* and happened to be doing a big UK tour at the end of the year too, so everything aligned, but in the end we were number two at Christmas behind the Flying Pickets' 'Only You'. 'My Oh My' reached number one outside Britain, but it was a shame we couldn't crack it at home as well.

However, it changed things for us because that Slade thing of 'something turning up' happened again. Just as we released 'My Oh My', Quiet Riot were having a top-five single in the States with 'Cum On Feel The Noize', and the record companies were aware of us again. Suddenly we'd got a new single of our own as well that was going to work on American radio, and 'My Oh My' hit the US top forty, the first time we'd done it. The planets were aligning for us over there at last. Or so we thought.

The success carried on into 1984 when we put out 'Run, Runaway' as the follow-up single and got a great response. Essentially, it was a folk song, a Scottish jig. Big Country were around at the time, and they were an influence on that record, and there's also a bit of 'You Ain't Seen Nothing Yet' in there too. I'm playing power chords mingled in with Jim's violin, and it makes this Celtic sound. We did a great video in a castle in Ledbury that went over really well on this new cable television station MTV. We had a caber tosser in it – the Americans love all of that – and had a top-twenty single in the States for the first time ever, so in March '84 we went back over the Atlantic to give it another go.

Sharon Osbourne was managing us over there by now, and so we had a run of support shows with Ozzy lined up after playing three warm-up club gigs. The record company was behind us, and it suddenly looked as if we were finally going to crack it after all those years of trying. We played our first gig with Ozzy at the Cow Palace in San Francisco and we had a real buzz going.

After the gig we went back to the Sunset Marquis Hotel just off Sunset Boulevard, which was where big bands always stayed, and Jim started to feel really ill – he said later that he thought he was dying. A doctor came in and diagnosed a severe case of the flu, but it wasn't that at all. Jim was laid up in bed for a week, so me and Nod got sent out on the road to promote the record, pending us getting back out and carrying on with the gigs again. But that never happened because it turned out that Jim had Hepatitis C, and we came back home to let Jim recover – he was sick for months. Sharon tried to get us back out to the States once he was well to follow up what we'd started, but our hearts had gone out of it. Me and Nod told her we felt we were flogging a dead horse.

America just wasn't going to happen for us – it wasn't meant to be – and as it turned out, the Cow Palace was it: we never played another full show as the four of us again. That side of Slade was over for good.

17

LET'S CALL IT QUITS

What we didn't appreciate when we turned our backs on America for the last time in 1984 was that we were also starting to bring down the curtain on Slade in the form of me, Don, Nod and Jim. It wasn't intentional, but the disappointment of the US trip being cut short then Jim being ill for quite a while took all the momentum out of what we had managed to recreate over the previous three years with the appearance at Reading and then 'My Oh My'. We weren't right down in the doldrums but it was hard to have had success snatched away from us again.

To make matters worse, we had a British tour tentatively booked for early '85, good dates in the Odeons and Apollos again, but we ended up cancelling that altogether. We'd never finally committed to it, but tickets went on sale anyway before it became clear in the last months of 1984 that Nod in particular wasn't interested in going back on the road. His marriage to Leandra was breaking down and this was affecting him really badly. He spoke to me about it, which I appreciated: 'You understand my marriage has broken down, and I can't possibly go on stage and be happy when my marriage is on the rocks.' I understood that.

Looking back, that was the beginning of the end, but we carried on in the studio and released *You Boyz Make Big Noize* in 1987. But without a tour to promote it, it didn't really do anything. That led to RCA dropping us. We were all doing more and more things on our own in this period. I was doing some writing with Bill Hunt, the keyboard player in Wizzard, and got Nod interested in working on the material. We went into the studio with Bob Lamb, who had been the drummer in the Steve Gibbons Band and had produced UB40's first album. Bob was a good guy and easy to be in the studio with. Nod came over and tried a song which I had written with Bill. Ruby Turner sang one part and Nod the other. It wasn't entirely the best song for Nod – it wasn't quite his range – but I was thinking what to do next, just trying to keep his interest.

Making *You Boyz Make Big Noize* hadn't been the easiest experience. We initially brought in Roy Thomas Baker, who had worked with Queen. He was very much into big production, working with lots of tracks on the recording desk and piecing things together. We spent three days just getting a drum sound for instance, which just wasn't us, and we struggled with it. Roy wanted to recapture Nod's original vocal sound, which Chas had always been great at getting. It's very much one or two passes at it with Nod. He's not the sort to sing things over and over again, but Roy used a number of microphones in different places and made him sing over and over to get the sound, and Nod became uncomfortable with this. The costs were escalating too, and in the finish Nod and I had to stop the sessions. The rest of the album was produced by Jim.

I think with the issues we had making that record, especially in terms of his own input, Nod was starting to question whether it was worth it any longer. With all the other things going on in his life, I don't think he felt like he needed the hassle. My motivation was just to keep him interested so that at some point we could all get back together and work as Slade again, though I think, looking back, Nod had already begun to drift away.

One day me and Nod were doing some Elvis Presley stuff, and then we did an arrangement for 'Crying in the Rain' by the Everly Brothers, which was really enjoyable because we loved that song. Polydor took an interest and wanted to put it out, but as Slade rather than just me and Nod. Then they wanted us to re-record it, but Nod refused because he felt he had done it as he wanted to, so it all fell by the wayside. That was really frustrating because I felt Nod was just finding his way back into the music at that point.

He'd gone through this spell where he had decided he was not going to play guitar for Slade, which was really odd because we were all about performance, playing together. I don't know whether all the stuff going on in his personal life and then in the studio knocked his confidence. But one day when it was just me and him in the studio he got a guitar around his neck and played like he did in the old days – he did some rock 'n' roll. We just let the tape go, and at the end I said, 'How good was that?' It was really good, and it was like he was himself again, really relaxed, enjoying himself, and his voice was so strong. But then came the delays with Polydor and maybe for him it was, *Oh God, here we go again.* In the end the single was released independently under the name Blessings In Disguise.

We didn't play again as Slade until 1991, when our fan club organised a convention for the twenty-fifth anniversary of the band. We did 'Johnny B. Goode' on stage in what remains the last time the four of us have played live together. Polydor got in touch later in the year to talk about a compilation album, *Wall of Hits*, asking us to produce a couple of new singles for it with the possibility of a deal for a new record if these singles worked out.

The first one came out in October '91. It was Jim's song 'Radio Wall Of Sound', with 'Lay Your Love On The Line', a tune I wrote with Bill Hunt, on the B-side. The fact that Nod didn't write any of it and then only sang on part of the A-side with Jim doing the main vocal was a good indication of where he was with the band by then. Actually it was a good record, but it didn't quite sound like Slade because Nod's voice wasn't prominent. The verse was too low for Nod to sing, it wasn't in his range, so we had Jim fronting it, and when we went on *Top of the Pops* people found that strange. We'd had a meeting at Jim's house trying to conjure up a look for the show, and it was all long leather coats and hats, and that really wasn't us. We looked like the Long Ryders or something, all in black, when we were all about colour.

It made it to number twenty-one, which was encouraging, and the hits album did decent business too – it went silver – but then we released 'Universe' as a single just before Christmas, same format with Jim's song on the A and 'Red Hot' by me and Bill on the flip. But this disappeared without trace, and Polydor backed off the idea of a new album. That was the final straw for Nod, although perhaps he'd already had enough anyway. Either way, in 1992 he came to us and said, 'I can't continue. I'll step down and let you three carry on.' I spoke to Jim about carrying on with a new singer, but I got the impression he didn't want to start all over again without Nod. After twenty-five years, Slade as me, Don, Nod and Jim was over.

It was a huge disappointment, twenty-five years together being over just like that, but I didn't have time to dwell on it. I was forty-six and needed to pay the mortgage! Being famous but broke is not a good option. Being famous and people thinking you're loaded when you're not is even worse.

My first thought was putting together a Dave Hill band of some kind, either going out live or maybe building on the songwriting I'd done with Bill Hunt, but I really wasn't sure about what to do. So I had a chat with Keith Altham, who had done some of our publicity way back, a straight, well-connected guy who had always been helpful over the years. We talked it through, and he put me in touch with one or two other people, and the sense I got from everybody was that if I went out again, if I was going to make it work, I had to make it clear that I wasn't just Dave Hill, I was Dave Hill of Slade. I would have to use the band name, and it seemed OK to do that when Jim and Nod had walked away. I hadn't pushed them; they'd made their own decision.

Right out of the blue, Len Tuckey, Suzi Quatro's husband, although they'd split up by then, rang me to ask what I was doing. We'd toured with Len in the past when he was in Suzi's band. I was talking about the situation when he said to me, 'Do you want to go out and earn £200 a night playing in pubs, Dave? You're mad. You've done all that. You're Dave Hill from Slade. You've got to go out as that.'

This was a reminder of what I had been a part of building over the years and boosted my confidence at a really important time. Len became my manager and was great for me because, like Chas, he cut to the chase. 'This is the way forward; this is how we are going to make this work.' He was very definite that me and Don could go out and play the songs under the name Slade. Len had the blueprint because he'd done it with Suzi. 'There are lots of places that would love to see you play. There are a lot of bands out in Germany, and they're not all original but they're still using their names – the Rubettes, the Searchers, the Tremeloes – loads of 'em, playing to big audiences. Suzi has never stopped working since the seventies.'

I went back to Jan and told her, 'I've just had this conversation, and Len has got me excited.' Then I rang

Don, who by this time was working behind the bar in a hotel that his wife was running. That was how desperate the situation was for him. His immediate reaction – he didn't need a second to think about it – was, 'I'm in.' So Don was on board too, and we were the two guys that had formed the original band. We were still Slade.

I called Nod to talk about it, and he said, 'I can't think of anybody better to manage you, Dave. Len's already been through it all and been successful.' I told him I'd come up with the idea of going out as Dave Hill's Slade, and Nod said he wasn't wildly happy about it, but, 'Dave, you have to pay the mortgage.' Then he said, 'Don't go out as Dave Hill's Slade, go on as Slade II. It'll indicate there's been a change but it still has the name.' Len was happy with that.

Then it was on to Jim, and there's no doubt he wasn't happy that Slade was going to carry on without him. I think Jim always saw Slade as the four of us or nothing, and he's entitled to that view, but in the end the simple fact was that Don and I had never left and had been left holding the Slade baby! As the years since then have proved, what we've done has only helped the Slade legacy, keeping the songs and records in the public eye, and I'd like to think that all four of us have benefited as a result. Meanwhile Len was great, because he was really reassuring. 'I've checked all this out with a lawyer and you have every right to use the name. That is who you are. Let's crack on.'

I was really missing performing. I've always loved playing for people, getting off on the excitement, and we hadn't played a proper gig since the support show with Ozzy Osbourne in March 1984. The prospect of being a live band again was just brilliant – I couldn't wait – so we got in a rehearsal room with a couple of guys that Len knew. They didn't actually end up joining us in the finish, but once Don sat behind the kit and we started playing, it was great, right from the first moment. That atmosphere was there. It was like we had never stopped playing together. Len said, 'There is something undeniably right about this.'

Eventually we settled on a line-up with Steve Whalley singing and playing some guitar, Craig Fenney on bass and Steve Makin also on guitar. I was dreading the reaction that we might get without Nod especially, but I felt like I was in a rock 'n' roll band again, although not quite back to the pubs. We played our first gig in December 1992 in Sweden to avoid any negative feedback from British fans, but once we got on stage, the nerves disappeared. It was as if we were young again! Then just after Christmas we did a show for this big German promoter, Rainer Hass, in front of 16,000 people. I don't think we were that great, but we were off and running.

We got offered an Australian tour early the following year, three weeks' work, which was probably the best thing we could have done because we needed the gigs to get us into real shape, however much we rehearsed, we got slagged off in the press – 'This isn't Slade; there's no Noddy Holder; it's a con' – some really disparaging stuff. Then it turned into six weeks out there instead of three, which wasn't ideal. I was missing Jan and the kids and wanted to come home, but it had to be done. We came through it and were so much better at the end. We played over eighty shows in 1993 and we were moving forward.

When we got back, Rainer offered us forty shows in Germany, and within a month C&A were using 'Far Far Away' as an advert for jeans, and it went into the charts. In Germany we travelled on a big tour bus with bands whose records I'd bought as a kid – the Tremeloes and Searchers. It was fantastic when you think of how low I'd been twelve months before. On the bus we were all mates – no egos, everybody had done it, we'd all got nothing to prove.

I was enjoying it, and the band got better and better. Len was with us all the time, looking after us and looking after the business, and that was invaluable. It was all just such a relief. Not only was I doing the job I love, I was also earning a living. Don was feeling good too. It was like being back with my family. All those years, and now I realised just how much family meant to me...

18

FAMILY MAN

There were some pretty turbulent years to endure and enjoy with Slade, right through from the time when success first hit us in the early 1970s on to that point when the original four of us went our separate ways. Through it all, especially from the real high point of 1973 onwards, my stability has come from family life, although perhaps I didn't make enough of that in those earlier years when I focused pretty much totally on the band and my career.

When you're in a group that's as hot as we were, you're hooked into a situation where you don't want to miss an opportunity, so you could be coming home after six weeks in America and telling your wife that in a week's time, a week that you'll spend getting over the jet lag, you're going to Australia. It's an unnatural way to live that affects you and those around you, who, as I realised later, are left behind to keep things going.

The big mistake I made was buying the house in Solihull. It meant Jan was isolated from her family and friends when I was away on tour. If she'd still been around the corner from them, she would have had people near her to talk to and to help her with Jade when she needed it. Because she lived so far from them – and remember there were far fewer motorways back then – Jan's parents weren't able to visit very often, and that put a strain on everyone. I know now just how great it is for me to be able to see my grandchildren whenever I want, and how good it is for my kids to know that they can drop their children off with us and go off to work or get on with other things. Jan never had that opportunity, and it took its toll on her.

In the later stages in Solihull, 1977, 1978, things weren't going well for the band, but we still had a mortgage to pay, so we were playing anywhere and everywhere that would have us, just to bring the money in. That meant being away from home without the compensation of making good money, and Jan was having something close to a breakdown, what she refers to as the period when she would be hoovering in the house and would suddenly break down crying. And when I was at home, I wasn't good at picking up on things because I was thinking about the next thing we had going on.

At one point, Barbara and Steve, a fantastic couple who made some of my stage clothes, moved in with us. They were very bohemian, very creative. Jan would come home to find piles of washing-up and material everywhere. It had seemed like a good idea, but rather than helping, having that, having our Great Dane running around and getting loose in the town, it was all driving Jan to distraction. It didn't help that I was in a similar state.

Around the time 'Everyday' was in the charts, spring 1974, I went to see a shrink because I was suffering from being cooped up in hotel rooms, that claustrophobia I've always had. And I didn't have any sense of perspective on things. It was always the band that came first, partly because I was enjoying it so much, but also because it was how I supported my family.

Jan was never comfortable with the rock 'n' roll lifestyle; she's very down to earth, very family orientated, and she didn't like the fact that everyone knew where we lived in Solihull, which meant we were always getting people knocking on the door. Nor did it help that every now and then she got caught up in the publicity machine. I've already mentioned the photo shoot in the bath, but that wasn't the only thing. Back in '73 for instance, we were keeping the fact that we were married quiet. That was what you did as a pop star then – you were supposed to be 'available' – but we were at a party at Jim's house and somebody noticed Jan's wedding ring and told a journalist. Of course they doorstepped her at work to get a quote. She ended up escaping through the shop next door to the hairdresser's where she worked. The following day they chased her down the lane near the house. In the end we got a heavyweight publicist, Les Perrin, to squash the story. The irony was that Jim had got married – we only found out from the papers!

Looking back at our time in Solihull brings a mixture of emotions. We had Jade when we were there so it will always be special. It was a lovely house, and both of us had dreams of buying it back later on, but at the same time there were periods when Jan was very unhappy. We didn't fit in socially with the plummy set down there and were vulnerable to being ripped off whenever we had things done to the place because people assumed I was drowning in money.

That was never the case, and very definitely not as the 1970s rolled on. After we came back from America and realised that we had been pretty much forgotten in this country, the money dried up and all of a sudden a lot of decisions had to be made. We needed to tighten our belts, and the house had to go. This was when the band was crumbling and we were asking ourselves, 'Where do we go from here?' The only answer on a personal level was to leave Solihull. It was sad in a lot of ways, but I think that moving back towards Wolverhampton, closer to our families, was ultimately good for us and especially for Jan.

But I was a bit impetuous again and bought a farmhouse near Albrighton. I looked at it with my dad, and it seemed ideal. It was set back from the road between two fields, and had some land and a barn, but even though it was nearer to everyone, it was still a bit out of the way. And I was still going away a lot, doing the Meccas and the like just to keep the band going, and Jan never really felt safe there. There was a long drive up to the house, and people kept driving down it and then turning round when they realised it wasn't a road.

Neither of us quite settled there. It had a cellar which was a bit creepy with a pump to keep it dry, and the boiler frequently went out. Basically, it was a 200-year-old house that needed work doing on it. We weren't particularly happy, although it was nice and rural with views across fields. Then in 1978/9 we had one of the worst winters ever; there were rats in the barn and mice in the house, and it was time to get out. Luckily it sold quickly and we even made a decent profit. That was a huge relief, as this was at a time when Slade were selling no records and the band was almost breaking up. It was a godsend.

We moved back to the Penn area and a sizeable 1930s semi with a big bay window. We walked in, and it was the first house that we both liked. It had a few features that put us in mind of Solihull. We moved in in 1980 and were just getting the house together when the whole Reading thing came up and put Slade back on the map. We'd come through a bad period and now we could look to the future again, so much so that we had Sam in the spring of 1981.

I remember Jim and Louise came over to the house and Louise said, 'I think you've found a home.' It was an interesting comment, and she was right. There was something homely about the house. It wasn't over-big, but it had character and the road was quite nice, mostly older people who had been there years. We ended up extending and extending it. Bibi was born in the autumn of 1982, and we became more of a normal family while we were in that house because, even post-Reading, Slade were never as busy in the 1980s as in the seventies, and from early 1984 we were off the road for the rest of the decade. It was my first chance to become really family-orientated, and that changed my outlook on life for the better. It was a very sweet time and gave Jan and me the chance to become much stronger as a couple, which is something I'm massively grateful for, because she has been my rock over the years.

Where I'm impetuous, will chat to anybody, and can be talked into doing all kinds of things, Jan is cautious and reserved. You have to earn her trust and her respect, and that's invaluable because I'll believe anything. Jan is always looking out for me. She understands how I operate in the world and clocks it all, working it out.

She's often introduced as 'Dave Hill's wife', which would get up anybody's nose. She is her own person, not an attachment to me. She's never warmed to the shallowness of the entertainment world, of being seen with the right people. Jan is very much about the family, us and the kids, the grandkids now, and we really built those foundations in that period in the 1980s when we finally settled in a house and I was at home.

Even then, financially it was a bit hairy at times, bringing up three kids as Slade was starting to come apart. It got to the point in 1988 where I was scraping the barrel a bit and I ended up having to get Sotheby's to come and look at my Roller with the YOB1 plate on it – they reckoned the plate was worth more than the car! They put it in a pop memorabilia auction with some old bangers that really were worth a fortune. It sold really quickly and that money came in at the right time. It really was like that at times, a bit hand to mouth.

Over those years I certainly tried to spend more and

better time with the family, but I'm not the most practical person, though I'm happy to get my hands dirty. That was literally the case the one time when the drains got blocked and I had to clear them out before I went to some fancy event in London. When I got there, I was greeted by, 'Well of course, you'll have come down in a limo,' but they didn't know that an hour before we set off I'd been elbow-deep in a crap-infested drain!

I must be frustrating to be around at times because I'm a bit clumsy – Bibi often says that they always had to come with me if I went into the garden to stop me falling in the pond or burning myself. I remember taking Bibi out for a walk when she was very young, and, as children do, she wet herself. My response was to go into a shop and buy her some new clothes – a pair of boy's boxer shorts and a T-shirt. For all that, I think between us we raised the kids well. Jan was the structured, disciplined one; I was more the the free spirit who encouraged them to express themselves.

The only real sadness during that time was that we lost Dad at Easter in 1986. He was in his eighties by then and he'd struggled a bit that winter, but as usual at Easter he went off to stay for a fortnight with Carol, who was living with her family in Hull. I took him to Birmingham and put him on the coach, and that was the last time I saw him in the sense of us being able to talk. Carol picked him up off the coach and he was a bit tearful – the journey had been a bit much for him. Then a day or two later he was unwell and fell, hitting his head on a radiator. Carol called the doctor, and it turned out that he had had two minor strokes, so he was taken to hospital in an ambulance. As they were getting him off the trolley onto the bed, Carol said all she could hear him saying was, 'Do you know my son is in Slade?'

He then had a heart attack and so I went straight to the hospital. I was looking at him and it was as if he was in a dream world. He hadn't gone, but he wasn't really there either. If he survived, which was very unlikely, he would be totally buggered, and Dad was never one to depend on me and Carol. He was always independent – with the dogs, playing his music and getting on with his life. Maybe he knew what the future would be and didn't want it? When he died, I went back to the hospital. It was something like one o'clock in the morning, and they had pulled the screen around his bed. His face was like porcelain – the colour had gone, there was undeniably nothing there. I know people are described as 'passing on' or whatever, but it wasn't like that. This was just the shell of someone I knew and loved. It really affected me. I kissed him on the forehead, and that was the end of it.

We eventually moved on from our semi in Wolverhampton in 1997, by which time the new version of Slade was well established as a working band and doing nicely, thank you. I was now earning good money, and at the same time I had some cash come in from elsewhere. As well as the mortgage on Solihull, I'd taken out an endowment policy at quite a few quid a month. That matured around then and gave us a really nice nest egg, and we were able to move to where we are now, in the same area but a bit bigger. I hated it when we first moved, but Jan saw the potential of it and the land the house had. She consulted an architect about what we could do and was full of ideas.

That was just as well because now we've got more space we can have open house for the family, the children and the grandkids, five of them now. We never went crazy with the band again after Jim and Nod left; we kept the schedule manageable and took our families with us whenever we could. Things are in much better balance than they have ever been. That's been a lifesaver for me, almost literally as it turned out later. Without Jan, Jade, Sam and Bibi and their kids, I don't know where I'd be.

19

SLADE ROCKS THE WORLD, AGAIN

One of the real joys of Slade's return as a gigging band since 1992 is that we've managed to see a hell of a lot of the world that we never got to back in the old days. It's given me the chance to meet some fantastic people, see some amazing places, and we have played to some extraordinary audiences, big and small.

At the smaller end of the scale, we played the town hall in Port Stanley. It was 2001 when we were invited to play in the Falklands. It was an eighteen-hour flight from RAF Brize Norton to Ascension Island, with the RAF themselves, to entertain the troops. It reminded me of the days of Vera Lynn in the war or Bob Hope going out to Korea, and I was caught up in the idea of it all, doing something for the country. The planes only fly out there once a week, so if you get stuck, you can't get back. People have been stuck on Ascension Island for ages. A military flight was a very different experience, very professional but no frills at all. They had these fat video players with a choice of films on them – we each had one of those, built to military spec. They looked after us really well.

England was cold when we left and Ascension Island completely the opposite – humid and warm. We had to spend several hours hanging around while they refuelled the plane, and then it was another long flight to the Falklands. It wasn't far from the airfield to the camp, which was a massive place with its own cinema and a huge gym with all the facilities, and all the entertainers were together – there was us, a girl singing group and a comedian.

The change in time zone was really hard to get on with. The first night we were there, we were all wide awake, and there were people wandering the corridors. I couldn't sleep so they moved me into the married quarters area, which felt like a mile away by the time I got there. It wasn't anything elaborate but it was really quiet. On the plus side, I lost quite a bit of weight with all the walking between there and the officers' mess. We ate with the officers, and it was a bit silver service. One evening we were invited to join the senior officers for an evening meal, and that was a jacket-and-tie job.

The idea was that we would play every night in the club on the base and then do one show in Port Stanley for the public. Getting from the base to Port Stanley was hazardous. A bit of bad weather and you wouldn't make it. You needed a seriously good Land Rover. I can only describe it as a bit like the Outer Hebrides it was so wild. A lot of the Argentinian mines hadn't been cleared, so you couldn't go to big areas of the islands, and you had to keep to the roads. Every now and again a sheep would explode a mine. They took us to the outskirts of it where it was all wired off, a bit like something you'd see in an old prisoner-of-war movie.

We had a night off to adjust, then the following day they arranged for us to go out and see Mount Alice. This is a radar station, and apparently a bunch of people had been up there for months. If you get bad weather there's no way in or out as it's too high for helicopters to land. Luckily, the weather was good so we got on this great big Westland helicopter. We had to wear all the gear, so it really did feel like we were on manoeuvres. When we got to the top, a message came to look out of the windows because 'They're waiting for you.' We looked out and there were ten to fifteen of them mooning us – including the women! We'd been told that they were going to dress up for us and had expected Nod lookalikes and so forth, but never mooning! We landed and they were so friendly. We'd heard that a lot of service people go out to do two years and come back with loads of money because there's nothing to spend it on, so having us there helped break up the monotony for them.

We were shown around the place, and some of the surveillance equipment was really interesting. We all had a few to drink but then a weather warning came through and we needed to make haste. If the weather worsened, we'd have to stay the night, so we were quickly back on the helicopter and taken down.

The next adventure saw us taken to see some warships in dock down Port Stanley way. Like at the radar post, we met people who had been in action twenty years before, and once again they didn't want to talk about it – you could see how traumatic it had been. They ran us through an exercise for when an attack is imminent. They set up all the guns and rocket launchers on a ship, albeit loaded with blanks, and took us through this drill. I felt something of what it must have been like to be there when they were actually fighting. There were a lot of senior people on the ship at the time, and they were very hospitable. I felt very patriotic about entertaining them, I must admit.

Back at the camp, the concert was good fun, they knew all of the songs. Then we set off to play the town hall in Port Stanley. It's the only place you can play off the base. It was an unusual audience. The vicar was there, sitting up the front with one or two dignitaries. They had laid chairs out, and that is not a Slade gig! We were all looking at each other in the dressing room thinking, *This could go horribly wrong!* so I changed our set to suit the occasion. We started off with something a little lightweight, and I have to say it went quite well. There were young kids there with balloons, and some of them got up and danced, and it became like a party. It was only one night, and we got away with it.

Because it wasn't wise to try to get back to the main base after the show, they had provided accommodation in some metal huts, like bunkers but a bit better than that. The army had them in case of the weather. Some of the lads took them up on the offer, but I didn't like the look of them, and fortunately there was a hotel down the road which I had found when I went out for a walk.

There were one or two fairly decent shops there and a Co-op. It reminded me of old seaside scenes, snapshots from the 1960s. I asked a few of the locals, 'What do you do in a place like this?' They said, 'We don't do anything, and it's nice!' You could come in from England on the plane, and they wouldn't have a clue what was happening in the world. In the officers' mess the newspapers were a week old. I don't remember watching TV when I was there, and there was no mobile phone signal. I remember we were having to use some system to make calls back home with money in the slot. It was like going back to the Britain that I grew up in.

After the gig I went back to the hotel, got into bed, but then there was a banging on the door, which turned out to be this local character who knew everything about everybody. 'Are you coming out?'

'I'm in bed!'

But he carried on, so I gave up, got dressed and went downstairs to the bar with him. It was like going to a village pub where everybody knows each other. I thought I might as well join in. The majority were English, and they were saying how much they liked living there, away from it all. It was a nice night.

Closer to home, what has been an eye-opener is exploring a lot of countries in Europe that we never really saw before – the Berlin Wall was still up when we were gigging, so we didn't get to see the Iron Curtain countries in the 1970s. But we also never went to Italy or Spain and didn't do a lot in Scandinavia; we mainly covered

Germany, Belgium, Holland and France occasionally, the countries where we were having similar success to at home. We went to Australia as well, and of course there were the attempts to crack America, but there was a lot of the world we never saw.

When Don and I went back with the new band, we found out that the old Slade hits had had an impact in the Soviet Union, East Germany, Poland and Czechoslovakia, all these places that we knew nothing about. We'd got no idea how popular we were there. But I've ended up going to more places with the new Slade than I ever did with Nod and Jim. The audiences are incredible, and we have played some amazing shows. We did the Olympic Stadium in Moscow to 18,000 and the next night played a private party in a restaurant for a businessman and just fifty people.

People weren't supposed to listen to Western music in the old Soviet bloc, but that probably just encouraged them! We seem to have been very important among young people and within the culture of the music scene there. A dissident writer, a bloke who the public loved but the communist authorities didn't, wrote about us, Deep Purple, Led Zeppelin and the way our music influenced kids there. We've had people come to see us, bringing paintings of the band, in tears just from meeting us. It was a really emotional thing to be a part of.

The funny thing is that songs that were never that big here are massive in Russia. I suppose they got to hear us on pirate radio, tapes smuggled in, bootlegs, all that, because our stuff was never released there back in the

1970s. I have been told that the authorities tried to jam Radio Luxembourg, to stop their own people listening to rock and pop music. Certainly in what is now Latvia that was going on. The promoter out there told me that when he was a kid the radio frequencies in the Baltic states were interfered with. They didn't want young people listening to bands like us. Kids weren't allowed to be teenagers, so they had to import pop culture. And it wasn't just about the music, it was how we looked, just like it was in the UK. We must have looked like we were from another planet! We genuinely had no idea about the impact of our music in those far-off worlds like Russia.

You go there now and look at the buildings from that time, and they reflect the mood of the communist period. It must have been so dull. They built monstrosities – big halls and dingy rooms. The hotels are different now, but when we first started going out there twenty years ago there was still a lot of rough stuff there. When you went out of Moscow or St Petersburg and went further afield, there was also a lot of corruption, but the audiences were brilliant, and they've remained that way as times have changed there.

Times change, fashions change, places change, but if you have good songs and you can put them across, if you can entertain your audience, you find that wherever you go people are the same. They want a good night out, a release from being at work all day, paying the bills, running after the kids. That's what Slade has always offered and always will.

20

MY HEALTH: LOSING AND FINDING JOY

When I started out as a rock musician back in the 1960s, it wasn't a profession that came with a guarantee of getting to your pension, and through the latter part of that decade and then into the seventies, the number of casualties was pretty frightening. I've had my brushes with ill health over the years too, though how much that's been a result of the lifestyle and how much just a consequence of how I am and who I am, and good and bad luck along the way, who knows?

I've always been a bit of a worrier. Looking back at my life while writing this book, I've come to think that dates back to my childhood and that maybe it's just in the genes. Certainly the guilt that Mom felt about all kinds of things, the feeling that you shouldn't have anything good happen to you, and that if it does it will be taken away, that is something I've carried on with me to some degree. I've had my brushes with depression over the years and have needed help in coping with it.

I've mentioned that I don't like being cooped up in small spaces, and over the years that's been a challenge because so much of my life has been spent living out of suitcases as I hopped from one hotel room to another. That wasn't so bad in later years when we had better control of our touring schedules, but in the 1970s, when we were constantly on the road, it did leave me feeling very low at times. In the later seventies, when the band was in trouble, we weren't selling records and were playing some terrible gigs just to keep going, it was hard, especially as Jan was suffering too. I know that Jim thought that I lost direction when the fame wasn't there, and I must admit I was affected by it winding down and thinking the band might not last.

In the late 1980s, early nineties I started to suffer from panic attacks. I could see we were falling apart as a band – that the end was nigh, if you like – and didn't know what I was going to do next, so I went to see a doctor. Funnily enough it was the man who'd bought my house in Solihull. I remember him asking my age and I said forty-something. He reassured me, saying it was common for this type of thing to happen in a midlife situation. 'You're not young, you're not old, and a lot of changes are happening to you. You're having to handle a lot of change.'

He didn't suggest I was going nuts, he saw it as something that I would get over but only with help, so I saw the odd therapist, and there was a woman called Claire Weekes who had made some self-help records which a friend lent to me. If you had a panic attack, you played one of these records, and she would talk you through it. One thing you shouldn't do with a panic attack is try to fight it. What she told you to do is really let go, rather than fight to get away, which only makes the panic attack worse. When you let go, you realise that the attack will not harm you, and that's really important because when they're happening, it feels like you're having a heart attack. They're really that bad.

My fear was that I'd go like my mom had, and I know Carol has always had that fear too. But gradually I got over them. They lasted about twelve months, on and off. If I had a drink or two, I'd be all right, but that wasn't the answer. Rather than fighting an attack, you had to let it dissipate. And they did.

Thankfully, the panic attacks have never returned, but that didn't put a stop to my worrying. I was always the one fretting about whether we were going to make the plane, what the hotel was going to be like, if everybody was going to be on time – all those things – and it only got worse when Jim and Nod left. I felt that things were my responsibility, that the buck stopped with me, even though I've had some great managers in Len Tuckey and then Hal Carter and now his daughter Abbie, who has been a godsend for me and has taken those worries off my shoulders.

If the panic attacks never returned, that didn't prevent me suffering full-blown depression later on, though again possibly that was triggered by age – I'd not long turned sixty – as well as other things. It came on around 2007 at a time when I'd been casting around for greater meaning to the whole question of life. That was something that had been a part of my thinking for many years, going back to the late 1970s and eighties. I grew up in the sixties, when that kind of spiritual searching was very much a part of the scene, the whole Maharishi thing with the Beatles, the way Eastern philosophies came into the mainstream, all of that.

I think that when you're creative, you do get those great, fleeting moments when you're writing or playing when you feel like you're in touch with something beyond yourself, and that's something that has always interested me. I've delved into many things over the years, including the standard sort of Christianity that we're accustomed to in this country; I've seen gurus; I've looked into Buddhism, all sorts of religions and beliefs, trying to find some kind of strength to help me make sense of the world. But, looking back, perhaps the hole that I was trying to fill was a symptom of depression rather than what I was looking for?

When depression really took hold of me in 2007, I suffered for a couple of years with it. It was a very black time. Without Jan, I don't know how I would have come through it all. I used to sit with her every morning, and she would talk to me just to get me on into the day. Every day she would go over the same stuff. She was brilliant.

It was the classic thing with people who are depressed. You fight it, you think you don't need help, you don't need tablets, you reject every kind of help because you think you should be able to handle it. I've read up a lot on it since, and so many people have the same kind of stories about what they went through.

What really kicked it off was a physical issue because I needed an operation for a double hernia. They did keyhole surgery on it, much less invasive than it used to be, but it still left me feeling like a big bloke had kicked me in the guts and meant it. A top man did the op, and he was brilliant, but I felt very weak afterwards and something tipped in my head. My career doesn't just involve playing a guitar; I'm very visual on stage, very active, very physical, and this operation, perhaps combined with turning sixty, made me start questioning myself. Over a period of time I lost confidence. I was nervous about kicking my leg up on stage – would it cause another hernia?

I had this in the back of my mind and then, shortly afterwards, I had a headache one day and I thought it was the sun. So, from nowhere, I suddenly had this thing about sunshine and wore shades all the time. Slowly that developed into a serious phobia and things just accumulated. Eventually, I went to see my doctor and initially we tried therapy, but I was completely confused. I'd be wide awake at two in the morning and couldn't go back to sleep and then be knackered for the day, so this professor in Birmingham, a psychiatrist, put me on this medication, which did sort of help – I took it at night and it did help me to sleep – but even then I felt it wasn't working, that's how confused I was at the time.

The professor upped the dose but I still said, 'This ain't working,' and he could see that, so I came off the drugs and felt absolutely shattered. The professor said, 'I knew you would be. I'm going to recommend that you see a colleague of mine who I went to university with, a practising psychiatrist.'

I put that off for a while because I thought I was going like my mom. *They want me to see a psychiatrist. I must be going mad.* I was looking at myself in the mirror and seeing an insane person. I was banging walls around the house and saying some strange things. My wife couldn't cope with it – she wanted to check me into a hospital – so eventually I went to see the psychiatrist and said, 'Look, I don't want any medication. I've tried it and it doesn't work.' So she said, 'Right, that's fine. Why don't you just tell me how you are, Dave.'

'I've lost my joy, I can't listen to music, I can't cry, I don't want to do the garden, I'm not enjoying anything, I can't feel anything, just a horrible blackness.' It was like that for an hour and a half and then I said, 'So what do you think?' She answered, 'Ninety per cent, you're depressed. I'm going to tweak your medication.' I thought, *Oh my God, here we go again*, but she was absolutely right, and the results are there to see. She's been great for me. She turned so many things around and got me seeing things straight again.

It wasn't plain sailing even then, and I wouldn't like to pretend it was because I know that other people are going through this right now and they need to understand it does take time, it has its ups and downs, but you have to believe there is light at the end of the tunnel. I'm still on medication. It's working for me and it has for the last seven years. It got me well, but it was a journey because there's a lot of confusion that goes with taking medication. But I was lucky in that I saw someone who listened to my concerns but was quite firm with me.

She said she had to tweak my medication, and I had to accept that. I would ring her up and say, 'It's not working, you know,' and she'd say, 'Just give it a bit more time, and anyway I'm going to increase it a bit.' Two weeks later I was thinking, *That old song was really good*, and I put this 1960s album on and it sounded great. Then I went for a coffee, which I hadn't done in ages, and a couple of days later bought a shirt, whereas before I couldn't choose. I couldn't make my mind up about anything.

The best analogy I can make is that it was like tuning up a car engine, and in fact I got better and better. Abbie said to me, 'What are you on? I want some of that!' I hadn't confided in her about my mental state at that time. She knew I wasn't right, and the band knew it as well, but we didn't talk about it. I was dragging myself on stage to perform, but if I hadn't gone on, I really would have been in trouble. The gigs did adrenalise me a bit, they did help, but the following day I would be down in the pit again. That went on for quite a long time and paranoia crept in. I felt people were talking about me, plotting. It was as if some exterior force was interfering with my life. Again that harks back to my mom 'This has happened for a reason.' Maybe. But I do know that coming out the other side of it was such a relief that I can't possibly describe it. It was like having my life back.

That wasn't the end of my health worries, and I guess that's inevitable as you get older. I'd been back to normal for around a year or so when in July 2010 we were playing a show in Germany and I had a stroke while we were on stage. It had started the day before but I didn't recognise what was happening. I was going dizzy but in an odd kind of way. Fortunately, it wasn't a major stroke, but it was big enough to cause problems.

Luckily, Sam was on the road with me, Abbie as well, so I had people around me. My son was worried to bits about me, but he was with me that night as I was taken to hospital, which was really good. They got the things round my neck and the screens going, looking for blockages, cholesterol build-up, all of that, and the doctor was explaining to Sam what he was doing. Then I was put to bed, and Sam prayed for me. I appreciated that because I was thinking, *It looks like it's all over then. All of it is out of my hands now.*

For the next couple of days it was test after test after test. Abbie came in at one point and – she remembers this well – I started to cry. Sam said, 'Get a grip, Dad,' and I said, 'I feel like I've let everybody down.' We'd had to cancel shows, and I might never work again. But after Sam told me the doctors said I was going to be OK, Jan had flown out and my initial panic was gone, I remember thinking there was no point in all the worrying I always did. It was a waste of energy. What good did it do? While you're worrying over little details, something big can happen to you – it could be a stroke, cancer, you could be knocked over by a car. 'Life is what happens to you when you're busy making other plans,' as John Lennon said.

Maybe the worry, that and the depression, perhaps it all contributed to the stroke, I really don't know –

obviously blood pressure relates to worry. Before I had the stroke I was avoiding getting things checked because I was afraid there might be something wrong. If my blood pressure was up, I'd put it down to the way I felt that particular day. And yet in hospital there was no escaping the tests, like it or not.

After they ran them all, they told me that I had had a stroke but a small one. They even showed me it on an MRI scan. Then they did a brain scan. There were all sorts of monitors on me, state-of-the-art stuff. All the things that I had avoided getting checked were now being investigated. And it was all good news, certainly compared with what I'd feared. They immediately put me on blood-pressure pills, statins, aspirin, the whole thing.

After three days I was allowed to get out of bed, and a physio came in to do things to activate my brain and work on my left arm, which had been affected by the stroke. No one said to me that my arm would be permanently damaged; it was a case of, 'You'll be OK but it'll take time.' They also put me on a diet. I lost a stone in the place because I got an apple, and that was about it!

I remember I went for a walk. It was a sunny day, so I was roaming around. It was a lovely hospital, they'd got a nice shop and a florist's. Simply because I felt like it I went into this shop to smell the flowers and it was like, *I'm alive! Whatever happens, I'm alive!* I was just elated. Then I went back to my room and they told me, 'We've done all the tests and we feel that we can release you.' All the people who had seen me came into the room. I hadn't met the main man before, but he knew me, he knew our music. He was like James Robertson Justice from *Doctor in the House* and he said, 'You play guitar, don't you? Well, don't worry, it will come back. Work at this.' There wasn't any negativity. 'I know what you do and it will come back.' What a contrast to what had happened to Mom when she damaged her wrist and was immediately told she'd never type again. That was the straw that broke the camel's back with her and sent her spiralling down.

The doctor told me that I needed to keep my brain active, that the circuitry in my arm had been damaged and it needed to repair itself. I said I liked coffee and asked if drinking it was good for me. 'As a matter of fact, that's very good because it alerts the brain. Keep drinking it!' The culmination of all this was that I was allowed out for a while before being released, and we went back to the hotel and had a nice meal together. I remember Sam had a few pints, just out of relief. He wasn't steady on his feet that night. But what really helped me was that there was a piano in the bar. The piano is not my instrument, but I can play, and I didn't want to attempt to play a guitar, not with my arm as it was – I couldn't even brush my hair.

The lady in the hotel said I could play the piano if I wanted, so I sat down and rested both my hands on the keys. I've written melodies on the piano and know people like them because I've played them in hotels in the past and they've said so, so I started to play what I remembered. Because my bad hand was resting on the keys, it wasn't having to support the neck of a guitar, so

I was managing and quite enjoying it. Jan was sitting in the corner, just having a drink. Then a nurse from the hospital came to take me back and he said that he played the piano, 'But I don't play as well as that.' That was really encouraging.

Later on, there was an ambulance booked to take me to the airport. The medics and I were in the ambulance, and Jan, Abbie and Sam followed in a taxi. As I was getting into the ambulance, the nurse told me that if I was worried about anything I should speak to my doctor because more often than not things could be sorted 'if we know in time'. That now made a lot of sense to me – had I thought that way before, maybe it could all have been avoided.

We were heading off and ran into a traffic jam on the autobahn. The ambulance pulled over to the hard shoulder and the taxi stopped behind. The two drivers had a chat: 'We've got to get him to the airport because he's got a plane to catch.' 'Whatever you do, follow us. Don't worry about the police.' So they put the blue light on and whisked me to the airport. It was a great feeling! I was in first class on the flight and Jan in business class. At Heathrow my driver picked me up and then we were home.

I knew that what happened over the next two or three months would be defining. My doctor at home told me that when people have a stroke, often you have the elation of still being alive, and then you get depressed when you think that things might not work out. I wanted to avoid that and just make things work, so every day I played the guitar, working my fingers using the exercises they had told me to do. I stuck with it. When we went on short breaks up and down England, I carted the guitar everywhere.

Jan then said I needed to get together with the band, so we booked some studio time and did a few tracks. I was still getting tired then. I would work for a time and then I would have to stop. What really worked well for me was to just go over the songs and then play the set. We found an out-of-the-way place and just bashed through it. Obviously I was thinking, *Can I still do this? Have I got the fire?* I wouldn't say I was note perfect but I certainly had the attitude.

Within just a few months after my stroke I had to walk on stage in Norway and do it for real, and Sam was in the same position at the side of the stage as he was when I collapsed, by the equipment. For him it was quite emotional. For me there was nervousness because I hadn't done a full set, but then adrenalin took over and I got on with it.

Partway through the set I told the crowd – everyone in Norway speaks perfect English – 'I had a stroke three months ago and didn't think I'd play again, but I've recovered and this is my first gig back. I can't think of anywhere else I'd want to be.' We were going down great, and I got a nice reaction, but it was the truth. I love Norway. From there I was easing my way back in, and before long it was back to normal.

Then again, what's normal? Nothing is ever plain sailing, and I was reminded of that in December

2016 when I had another accident that could have been disastrous. We'd played the last show of our UK Christmas tour at Brighton and had a brilliant night. The following morning my driver was going to pick me up from the hotel, so before breakfast I went out for a walk on the promenade, feeling great, looking forward to going home and enjoying Christmas.

I was walking on the promenade when suddenly, *whack!* A cyclist had ridden into with me, and I'd been knocked down onto my left arm. It didn't hurt, it was more the shock of it. There was a girl standing over me, saying, 'I'm really sorry!' Her bike was on the floor, and a couple of joggers helped me up, and to be honest I didn't really know what had happened. They asked me if I wanted to go to hospital, and the girl tried to straighten my arm. It looked OK, and I thought it was all right, so they left and I walked on for a bit. Then I tried to bring my arm back towards my chest and I heard *clunk*. It wasn't just a pain, there was movement, so I knew something was properly wrong.

I went back to the hotel and bumped into Robin, our sound guy. I must have looked a real mess because the side of my face had been bashed as I fell and I'd ripped my coat. I looked like I'd been assaulted. He got me a taxi to hospital and they did an X-ray. The doctor told me, 'It looks as if you have a displacement in the elbow. It'll probably require an operation to put a pin in.' I wasn't going to have it done there, so they put me in plaster and I came home. But this was 23 December, and with Christmas coming I had to wait for the new year to see anyone.

I got that all organised and went into hospital to see the surgeon. He got the X-rays up and said, 'I'm sorry, but this is a very, very serious break. It'll be a very delicate operation because of the position of the nerve, and I can't guarantee that you'll get the full movement back.' Immediately I thought of my mom and that wrist injury, the doctor telling her she'd never work again. That flashed through my mind. But after he told me there was a bit of damage to my wrist as well, he still hadn't finished. 'The other issue is that I know you've had a stroke in the past. I can't rule out the possibility of you having another one.' That was the icing on the cake! But really there was no option, because without the operation I would never get full movement back, so we had to plough on.

The good news came at the end when he said, 'I can do the op tomorrow if you want me to. I've had a cancellation.' My reaction was immediate: 'Get on with it then!' Rather than going away and worrying about it for a couple of weeks, I'd get it over and done with. My other concern was being knocked out, because the last time I'd had an anaesthetic, for the hernia operation, that was what started the depression. But he said, 'It's too risky for you to have a local. This is a tricky operation, and I don't want to run the risk of you moving while I'm doing it.'

So I went in the following day, went under the anaesthetic, and the next thing I know, I woke up and said, 'My God, I'm in hospital! And I'm still alive!' I was just elated not to have had a stroke. Unfortunately, it took a while for me to come round, and the surgeon wasn't available to talk to me immediately, but Jan went off to find somebody to tell us how it had gone, and it transpired that everything had gone well.

I went home that night to rest for a week, and then it was on to physio with a guy called Jaspal, who was brilliant. He was very calm but very strict. It didn't help that every time I went to see him, Jan stitched me up: 'He hasn't been doing his exercises properly.' But I put the work in with him, and gradually I was able to do more and more things and to start playing again.

Jan helped by buying some extra-large T-shirts and jumpers, which she'd zip me into with my left arm inside so I couldn't do anything with it, because it drives you mad not being able to take the lid off a jar or something and you keep trying when you shouldn't. I'd also just taken delivery of a beautiful new guitar – I'd only been waiting five years for it – and there it was sitting in the house at last, and I couldn't touch it!

I also had a belt that strapped the arm to my side so I couldn't move it during the night, all to help make sure that it healed properly. It was awkward because having only one arm affects your balance even when you're doing normal things like going for a walk, which I do regularly. It made it a real job to escape from a herd of cows chasing me, but that's another story...

With all these trials and tribulations, I've been so lucky to have great people around me to make things work and take care of me, especially Jan and Abbie but also the guys in the band too, Don, John Berry and Mal McNulty. I've had to do things a little differently though, especially as a consequence of the stroke. Jan and Abbie worked hard to get me less involved with all the little things that I used to worry about so I can just turn up, play, and have nothing else to concern me. Abbie has been so good at taking those things on for me, and that has made a huge difference.

The stroke really changed me. I realised just how vulnerable I was to damaging myself, to almost literally worrying myself to death, to believing things, to relying on other people. I looked back at those years when I was looking for answers and realised that I was searching for something to rely on, a crutch if you like. But after the stroke I found that the strength I had always been looking for was inside me. That doesn't mean I don't believe in anything any longer, and I think that religion can be great for other people, but going to church and meetings and all of that, that's no longer for me.

The stroke was a reality check, and I came out of it to a better place – not that I would recommend a stroke to get there! My doctor has known me for thirty years, and he says I am in a better place now than I have ever been.

I do look at things differently since I had the stroke. I don't get worked up about things anymore. If I miss a flight, I miss a flight. Don especially will remember how I used to be a nervous wreck over the tiniest details. But, as Jan has often said, 'What are you so fussed about?' She's right, as usual.

21

FIFTY YEARS OF SLADE AND COUNTING

As Slade II, we played our very first gig on 11 December 1992, some twenty-five years ago. I've been in this version of the group, in one way or another, for as long as I was with Nod and Jim, longer as a proper working unit given that Slade didn't play again after March '84, when we left America after Jim got ill. It's been a huge part of the journey of my life, one I've continued to share with Don as well as a number of other musicians.

Early on, we became a five-piece with Steve Whalley singing and playing guitar, Steve Makin on guitar too and Craig Fenney on bass. Craig was replaced by Trevor Holliday after about eighteen months, then Steve dropped out of the group in 1996 and we stayed as a four-piece from then, which is a format I really like. Dave Glover came in and played bass after Trevor left in 2000, and then John Berry took over in February 2003 and has been with us ever since. Steve Whalley stayed until June 2005, when Mal McNulty came in as our lead singer, playing guitar too, and that line-up has been together since then, for over twelve years now. We are a really tight unit, musically and as people.

We've gone through managerial changes too. Len Tuckey was brilliant for me. He got the new band up and running, and made us believe in it, but there came a time when he wanted to step down. I needed someone who was going to be out there on the road with me, so Len put me on to Hal Carter, who ran an agency sorting out some of our gigs in Britain and Norway. To replace Hal, his daughter Abbie was put forward by both Len and Hal, and I think it was Jan who said, 'Give her a go.' It was a learning curve at first, but Abbie has been great. She's so organised and has taken all the old worries off my shoulders.

I would say that more than anything since my stroke, she has been someone who I can trust, because if she sees something that needs doing, she will do it. She had conversations with Jan after my stroke and I think she has just made the whole process more enjoyable by taking away the things that I would have to be dealing with in the past. Nowadays, I can go out to the show the day before, have a good night's sleep, go and enjoy myself, play the gig and know that she will look after the promoter and anything else that needs dealing with. That's a nice feeling to have after all these years.

There was a time when I thought that the original four of us would play together until one of us dropped, but that wasn't to be, although Don and I are still going on stage together more than half a century since our first gig with the Vendors at the Three Men in a Boat in Walsall on 3 January 1964. For us – and for a lot of Slade fans who had never had the chance to see the original line-up – it didn't end when Jim and Nod left. It's still going really strong.

I didn't know whether I could continue the group without Nod. It was like the Stones playing without Mick Jagger. Nod has a fantastic voice and very few people sound like him, though Steve and Mal have done a great job for us over the years. But what we did have going was the fact that, with Nod, I was the face of the band. People recognised the look and knew my personality, and so I had to trade on that and be even more front and centre than in the past. Not that I minded that!

Since I made the decision to continue with Don, we have been continually surprised at what turns up. Not only have we done regular gigs, we've also played shopping malls: Sweet on a stage at one end, someone else on another, a beer garden in the middle, the windows are rattling – it's all going on! To have gigged in Russia, in Latvia, in the Falklands – how did that happen? Or to find myself playing for a rich man in Russia because it is his fiftieth birthday, and there are a hundred people in the place and he just wants to listen to one of the songs twice before we do our set!

It has been such a great ride into the unknown and it hasn't mattered whether we're playing to a hundred people or twenty thousand people, all the shows have had a fantastic feeling to them. It's people all smiling, enjoying themselves, getting into the music, the playing, having a great time. To still be able to generate that excitement now, I'm absolutely thrilled about it and long may it continue.

The root of it came early on for me when Len Tuckey once said, 'The thing is, Dave, you are an entertainer.' He was right. It's not just about playing a guitar – I know I can play and I know I have a feel for a melody – I also know that when I'm on stage there's something inside me that drives me to engage with people. It's like an electric charge goes through me as soon as I walk into the lights. You get to the side of the stage, there's that moment when you're waiting to go out and you don't know how it's going to go. Is it packed? Are they in a good mood? Are they on their feet down the front already? It's always a blank canvas every night, it could go any way. So my attitude is to walk out and, right between the eyes, 'Here we are. Get down and get with it!'

I know exactly what our fans want. They want to relive their past, their youth, their childhood. It is such a privilege to be a part of these people's lives, such a big part that all these years down the line they still want to give up an evening and come out and see Slade play. I can see how much it means to them.

It's a humbling experience to meet so many fans, whatever their background. The one guy we did a show for not so long ago, I think he was three times a billionaire and one of the nicest blokes you could ever meet. He came into the dressing room and was like a kid in a sweet shop. He wasn't swanning around doing the big I Am, he was just a fan. It was like if I'd met the

Beatles, the thing that mattered most in the world to me when I was a teenager. I've also loved playing to fresh faces too. Visiting Eastern Europe has been a thrill, and finding out just how important our music was for young people living behind the Iron Curtain. They knew our records but never saw us. Now they can see us play.

Despite the antics and the costumes, Slade was a proper band. We were always serious about what we were doing and didn't make under-par records. They were worked on; they'd got atmosphere; they'd got melodies; they'd got character, and that's why they endure. They didn't come off a production line, and they still stand up. It's not like I'm just trying to earn a few quid out of a bunch of embarrassing records. There are some really good songs which have lasted as well as early Beatles stuff. I'm just happy to be keeping Slade alive for so many people who still want to see and hear us.

22

SO FAR, SO GOOD

Just as my life has been a journey that's unfolded in these pages, so writing this book was a journey of its own. I approached it by wanting to answer a few questions I had about my life, my parents, my health, Slade, about how I got to where I am now. What was the real story of my mom and dad? Why were Slade such a huge success and why didn't we emulate that in the States? Where did my depression come from, and how did I survive that and my stroke? Those were all things I wanted to think more deeply about and, in doing that, in researching, in talking to people who have been involved in my life along the way, things have become clearer. As you'll have discovered by reading this book, I haven't got all the answers – I don't think anybody ever has – but a lot of things have come into sharper focus for me.

Going back over my childhood took me back to a Britain and a way of life that seem a very long time ago now, a life that was very much in black and white, just little bits of colour peeping out of the post-war austerity. It's a world that is long gone, but reflecting on it for the book brought home to me that while people associate me with the 1970s, I was very much a person formed by the 1940s and fifties.

It was a time where you had to wait for everything; there were no instant fixes like there are today. Wartime rationing of some items carried on into the 1950s, and you had to make do – that might account for why I was so impetuous later on – and appreciate what you had. Nothing was served up on a plate.

As with everything, there were good aspects to that and there were bad. I remember being happy as a child, but from the vantage point of 2017, it seems amazing that almost nobody had central heating. My bedroom was freezing, and in the winter you'd see crystals of ice on the inside of the windows. The idea that you could have a phone in your house, never mind one in your pocket, never occurred to us. Why would it? If you wanted to telephone, you walked to the phone box. That was how life was. My parents had grown up in Edwardian Britain, their parents were Victorians. This was still the era of the British Empire, the stiff upper lip, respect for your elders and for authority. I suppose one irony of my life is that when we were at our commercial peak in the early 1970s, Slade were the epitome of a modern, changing world.

Going back and thinking through those times, about the growth of the welfare state after the war, when we kids got free orange juice and that malt concoction to give us vitamins, has been a reminder of how things have changed, of how far we've come but also some of the things we've lost, most notably a sense of community.

That was something I definitely grew up with on the Warstones estate, everybody looking out for one another. I think it was partly a hangover from the war, but it was also because the people there were living a working-class dream in new council houses. The slums were in the past, you had indoor toilets and fitted kitchens and all sorts – this was the life!

Ultimately, it was the growth of the consumer society and that bit of affluence that came with the rebuilding of things in the 1950s that paved the way for the first generation of real teenagers to come through, and I was a part of that. In the fifties you looked like your parents, you dressed like your parents, your ideas and your way of looking at the world was formed by your parents, very often you even ended up going to work where they did. But by the time I left school – even though Mom got me a job – we were into the 1960s, and kids were starting to look for some independence, although I'd already had a taste of that at home anyway, mainly because of the circumstances surrounding Mom.

I've described some of the things that happened in our house while I was growing up. Looking back from fifty or nearly sixty years on, it is difficult to put myself in the position of a child experiencing his mom pretending to have strangled herself and taken a load of pills, seemingly because he accidentally put a brick through a window. At that age, you're not equipped for things like that. As I've said, the problems she had ran very deep and went a long way back, because I found those letters from her to her sister, written not long after I was born, that said she would have ended it all if she hadn't got me to look after. That's heavy stuff to carry, and I'm glad I didn't know about it when I was younger.

I still remember being really proud of her when I was young because I'd see her coming home from work looking so smart. The neighbours were all impressed with her too, but they knew that she'd have a secret drink in the back garden, which again I didn't known about until later. Most of the time life was just the normal day-to-day stuff, but every now and again something would happen and there would be pandemonium. And yet things that you'd think might set her off, like when I broke into the school and told her the police would be round, focused her. She realised the teachers and the police had been wrong to interview me on my own and dealt with them very calmly and with authority.

As I became a teenager, I just wanted to fit in, be like everybody else, and the fact that my mom was different, that she had these episodes, embarrassed me. Don't forget, this is the 1960s, into the seventies, and mental illness was something people didn't talk about, it was something to be ashamed of. People talk about it carrying a stigma even today, which may be true, but we've come a very long way since those days. It's far more out in the open, much more talked about, and treatment is better. Going back forty or fifty years, this was taboo stuff and you kept it as quiet as you could.

I suppose that although I knew ours was a slightly strange household in that sense, it was what I grew up with, it was all I knew, and we all got on with it. Mine was a happy childhood and I wouldn't want people to think otherwise. But having delved back into that period to write this book, I've realised that I talk about my mom in very different ways to how I speak about my dad, and I suppose I did have different relationships with them – and of course Dad was around for another ten years after Mom died, so we had longer together.

In Mom's later years, when she was in and out of the hospital and so on, I was distracted by the band, which was really full-on from the late 1960s right through to when she died in 1976. Carol saw a lot more of the problems, being younger and still living at home full time until late 1973, when she got married. I knew about what happened because Carol would tell me, but I didn't go through it.

I'm also now coming to recognise parallels between myself and my mom, but also points where we went off in different directions. The turning point for Mom was when she injured the tendons in her wrist, which stopped her going to work every day. I now see how important holding down a job and being respected and admired at work was for her emotional wellbeing. Once that was taken away, it accelerated and deepened the depression she suffered from, and she went into an irreversible decline.

For me, being in the band, being on stage, being in Slade, has been as important to my wellbeing as going to work was to hers, and when that has been threatened, I've suffered too. Fortunately, I've come through that, and then my stroke later on, in a positive way. How much that's down to me being a different kind of person, or how much it's that thirty and forty years on, treatment for depression and mental health issues has vastly improved, both in terms of medication and care, being treated at home and not by electric shock in the nut house, I can't say.

Certainly I wouldn't have wanted to go through what she did because the mental hospitals she was in were like prisons. I remember them as frightening, barbaric environments. I think that affected my relationship with Mom too, because I hated going to see her at Stafford. I wanted to see her, but when I got there I couldn't wait to get out. You'd see patients who were very ill. They'd shout at you just because you were a stranger. I was very uncomfortable there and resented having to go, much as I wanted to see her.

I was very much the typical teenager once the music came along – I went my own way and didn't care what my parents thought – and Mom and Dad allowed me to get away with it. Although I thought my parents were strict – we probably all do – when I started seeing Jan and she would come to the house, she couldn't believe just how much me and Carol were getting away with and how we could do what we wanted. Jan always used to say the kids were in charge of our house. She came from a much more traditional set-up, a loving environment but one where the parents laid down the rules and that was it. It wasn't quite that way with us.

Carol and I are both strong personalities, but I think it was that Mom wasn't always there mentally, and Dad was both preoccupied with taking care of that situation and happy to see us off doing other things and not being dragged down by it. He let us escape, though I can imagine now how worried about us he must have been. You're very self-absorbed as youngsters and don't think of others enough. When Jan came over, Dad used to love coming to the pub with us, not that he was a drinker. Now I can see that it gave him a bit of respite, but back then I just wanted to be alone with my girlfriend. The one time we didn't take him with us, he came marching down to the boozer and we had a terrific row about it. Thinking about it now, he was probably just upset that we couldn't see how much he enjoyed that little break from having to care for Mom. The truth was that I wasn't really bothered about anything beyond Jan and the band. I escaped from a lot of the things that happened at home by playing up and down the country, and subconsciously perhaps that was why the group was so important to me.

One difficulty I've faced in writing this book is that I want to speak well of my mom. I'm not angry with her, I love her, I understand she wasn't well, it wasn't her fault. I try to hold on to those times when she was well and don't want people to come away from reading this thinking that in any way she was a bad mother. She certainly wasn't. She was ill. That's why my relationship with her was more detached

I lost that normal mother–son relationship because, while Dad was always able to help me out, he'd fix the van or be there to give me advice or whatever, Mom couldn't. In later years, Mom would have been great to have around to look at documents and contracts, because she was smart, she understood business, and we could perhaps have become closer again that way. But we had just reached a point where we were living around her problems and then she was gone.

I really regret that she couldn't appreciate the success I had with the band because she wasn't mentally present enough by then. Dad was loving it all – he'd sign autographs and befriend fans – but it kind of washed over her. Like anybody, I wanted my parents to say they were proud of me. I wanted their approval and I couldn't really get hers in the end. That left something in me unfulfilled.

Towards the end she became a shadow of herself. There are pictures of her late on, and she looks like she's somewhere else. When Jade was born, Jan used to put her on Mom's lap and she'd hold her, but it was like she was thinking, *What do I do next?* Jade would start crying because there was no connection. That's how empty she was by then. This was the woman, remember, who had told my dad that she would love to have his children when they got together. But by the time her grandchildren arrived she couldn't feel anything for them.

When she died I didn't cry, and I do still wonder about that even now – that's one of those puzzles that I've tried to make sense of in this writing process. Slade were still busy at the time, but even so I don't remember ever feeling like I needed to come crashing down in tears about it. Jan says that's a classic tactic of mine though. If I don't want to deal – or can't deal – with something, I find a distraction and ignore it. Slade, recording, gigs,

America – that was all happening, and it seemed far better to lose myself in that than think about Mom. That's all true, but for years I just hadn't been able to have a close relationship with her. It's sad that we weren't closer, but I don't think it could have ever been any different. I understand that.

I remember feeling that her death would be a relief for Dad, because he'd had to deal with absolutely everything, and it was a right mess towards the end. He was a strong bloke, but I thought that would be a weight off his shoulders. But then I remember finding him in the front room staring at the ceiling and he said, 'I really miss your mom.' But I guess he was missing the mom that he had had the fake wedding with. I wish I could have seen that mom more than I did, because the two of them sound a lot of fun back then.

My life story is one of social change as well. To suddenly come across the fact that your mom and dad had arranged a fake wedding is mind-blowing stuff. I was talking to my aunt Hilda's son Gerald, and he just came out with, 'And of course there was the fake wedding.' 'What? A fake wedding? What are you talking about?' This was a bombshell, I had never heard of this before.

That happened because it was a different time with a different morality. Nowadays, people think nothing of an unmarried couple living together, even having children, but in the 1940s that was taboo, as was the fact that Mom had already had Jean, something she kept from Dad for quite a long time. Finding out about the fake wedding was extraordinary. I was shocked, but I certainly wasn't upset. I actually thought, *Good for them!* To do something like that, to pull the wool over people's eyes, not for any bad reason but simply because they loved each other and that was what they had to do to be together, was actually lovely. Very romantic!

It also made me look at them differently, not as 'Mom and Dad'. It helped me see them as real people making their way in life: Dad as the young adventurer who'd come back from Australia and was then willing to leave his wife because he wanted to have children and she didn't, Mom as somebody who had a wilder side to her, who was pretty, liked make-up and clothes, who wasn't always a woman so troubled by life and what had happened to her that she had been broken by it. There had once been a young girl there who was trying to put the past behind her and embark on a better future.

Yet what they did was possible back then: you could run away and start again if you wanted to. You could pitch up somewhere new, tell people the story you wanted them to believe, and that was that. Nowadays you're visible, your life is tracked. If you move somewhere new, the neighbours can search for you on Facebook, look you up on Google. Your past is something you can't get away from, like it or not, and it isn't always what actually happened either. Back then lives could remain mysterious, even for the most innocent reasons.

The fact that they did something as theatrical and extreme as stage a fake wedding so they could be together, perhaps explains why they were so willing to let me and Carol do our own thing when we grew up. If they'd done something so off the wall, how could they stop their children doing what they wanted? And certainly once I left Tarmac, they allowed me to go my own way. There was no 'There's no future in the guitar, stick to a steady job!' They let me really go for it, all guns blazing, no half-measures. Not that I knew about the wedding at the time, so I couldn't throw it back at them, but I wouldn't have had to anyway.

My parents certainly got the timing right as far as I was concerned, because I grew up listening to some great music – the Shadows, Buddy Holly, Chuck Berry. They all influenced me: their songs were where I got the chords from, they were the people I wanted to emulate, and then of course the Beatles came along and took it on again. Before that our house was like everybody's. You had Sunday lunch with *Family Favourites* on the radio, all that Glenn Miller, Bing Crosby stuff.

Music changed so much, so fast, but was still very much a gamble when it came to taking it up as a career. Certainly there were no guarantees of success because nobody really knew what success looked like for rock groups at that time. Ringo thought the Beatles would only be around long enough for him to make enough money to buy a hairdressing business! By then some members of that first wave of rockers like Jerry Lee Lewis, Chuck Berry, even Cliff and the Shadows to a degree, weren't as popular as they had been. Would they be able to carry on for twenty years, thirty years, a working lifetime, or would they have to go back to an office job or run a pub or go and work in a factory?

But that's the great virtue of being young – you don't worry about tomorrow. Now I look back and think how fearless we were. Early on, we just focused on the next step. There was a venue in Wednesbury we wanted to play, then wouldn't it be great to play Mothers in Erdington? Could we do gigs in London? Could we make a record? Would it be a hit? Could we record a number one? Can we get another one? These are all staging posts along the way. It's only later on, when you've lived a bit, had a bit of success, when you've got a lifestyle to protect, that's when the worries come!

I've had ups and downs over the years and I've tended to look at my life in terms of successes and failures, but I've come to realise that it's not like that really. Those things that I got worked up about and had sleepless nights over in the past – things going wrong, the way the money we earned was split, how the original band came to a close – I've got past them and I'm content. I've come to understand that where I am now, with Jan, with the children, the grandchildren, that's where I was meant to be, and it's a very good place.

The contentment I have now centres around what I've got, not a craving for what I haven't got. Bitterness doesn't do anything but eat away at you, and my view is that all the good and the few bad things that have happened along the way have led me to this place, so it's been worth it. I'd rather think about something Chas once said to Nod: 'We've had a great time, haven't we?' And we did, we had a fantastic time, and I'm still having a fantastic time. And writing this book has helped. Those great times are now front and centre in my mind when I think about the original four of us, not the fact that we broke up in the end. I think that's the only way forward.

It was very hard to feel that way when things weren't going well, and in the late 1970s I did find it hard to come to terms with not breaking America and the loss in popularity that followed when we came home. The popular version of the Slade story goes, 'They went to America, had a really miserable time and came back.' And I tended to buy into that as the years went by: 'Yeah, it was terrible.' But again, standing back now, there were a lot of things about that time that were great. It was interesting to experience living in a different culture, that alone was fascinating, but there were wonderful moments too, including playing some happening shows to receptive audiences.

What we maybe don't appreciate over here is that America isn't one big country; it's this bunch of very different places and identities, all with their own ideas, under this big umbrella of the United States of America. Go to New York, and it hasn't a lot in common with somewhere in Florida or Arizona or Arkansas. We found places like New York, St Louis, Fresno, other places too, where they loved us. We would go down a storm and sell records, but then we'd go elsewhere and they wouldn't have a clue who we were. They weren't into our kind of music and we couldn't get anything across to them. That seemed strange because in Britain, if you do well in Newcastle, you're likely to go down well in Bristol too. But we did make an impact in some places, and we still have a following out there. We get plenty of messages to the fan club from the States, and that's really nice.

I now see that it was when things began to fall away that I started to look for something beyond the group. Nod said I was the first one of us to stand outside the box. I was searching for something less material, and this was also perhaps a way of coping with what was wrong within the group. I needed something to feed that part of me. Slade had been such a big part of my life that when we stopped working so closely together, when we were no longer so tight as people, I needed something to fill that void.

It was a void because from 1971 through to 1974 we barely had a day off. If we weren't playing, we were recording. If we weren't recording, we were doing a TV show. If we weren't doing that, it was a photo shoot or being interviewed. We were everywhere from *Jackie* to *Melody Maker* to the *News of the World*. It was one high after another and another, and you can get used to that. It's a permanent adrenalin rush, and when it disappears, you need to replace it with something else. That's why so many people in the music business get into drugs and drink, though thankfully that was never my scene. I looked for a different meaning to life, and when you do that, it can be beneficial but can open up a lot of things best left alone too, and I think that played into my later depression.

I went through various spiritual journeys but ultimately came back to family and life's simplest pleasures – weeding the garden, going for a walk, playing the guitar for the joy of it rather than as practice. The stroke certainly accelerated my progress along that route and helped me realise that I don't want any structures confining my thinking. My feelings are very much between me and something bigger, without anything coming in between. The spiritual side runs deep in me, and I've found that connection in nature.

Quiet contemplation has come to mean a great deal to me after a life that was pretty hectic once upon a time and still can be. I take a lot of pleasure from reading Wordsworth when he talks about the elements, the 'whistling hawthorn', things that envelop experience. Being still enough in my own mind, clear enough to see the sun sparkling on the water, that matters to me now. You can have your mind so cluttered with things that you miss it, but when it does cut through, you get moments of clarity when things fall into place, even for just a moment. That was a sensibility that always ran through the band actually, even if we didn't recognise it. You get it in the yearning of 'Far Far Away' for instance. In a sense, coming from that to the way I look at life now, things have come full circle.

When it comes to Slade, taking a step back, I've come to realise just how hard we worked – just looking through the list of gigs we did in some years was exhausting – and how luck played an important role too. Finding Don right at the start of my musical career, bumping into Nod when I was looking to form a new band, Jim being at home that night when we went round to see if he was going to be right for the group, coming across Chas when we were starting to get into the studio, being invited to replace Ozzy at Reading when we were at our lowest ebb, Jim falling ill as we were just getting a foothold in the States, Len Tuckey telling me to use 'Slade' for the new band – all chance. However much you try to control things, other things crop up and change your path.

Twenty-five years on from Jim and Nod leaving, I've got a better perspective on the original Slade. When you have success and then it goes, you wonder what you're doing wrong, why isn't it happening anymore. But there's a bigger picture in music. Fashions change: kids don't want to follow the same group that their big sister or big brother loved – they want their own group. When you're seen as a singles band, then you're especially vulnerable to that in a way that, say, Pink Floyd or Led Zeppelin weren't. It's little to do with whether you're making better or worse records, more that a new group of record buyers wants the next new thing – as does the press.

I can't pretend that it didn't hurt when Jim and Nod went their own ways, because it did. I thought there was more music in us, that we could make some great records, that there might be another Reading Festival moment for us. Perhaps there would have been, who knows? We had a very special bond, we achieved some amazing things, made some great records, played some great shows. Closing the book on that was sad, and there was some anger there at the time too, because initially I couldn't see what life was going to be like without them and without Slade.

But as Jan said, I can detach myself from things. If I don't want to confront something, I turn my back on it and hope it goes away. And I suppose I did that a bit with Nod and Jim, but I couldn't afford to dwell on them leaving because I had to get on and make a living. So I threw myself into the next chapter, what turned out to be the next version of Slade, which has brought me just as many great moments and memories. When we first went out, I did question whether the new band was going to be good enough – I did carry that weight for a while – but over time I proved to myself that what I'd done before was good, that with me and Don the power of the band was still there, that I still had worth and that I could become a band leader too. Those things are satisfying to look back on.

The fact that we've had so much success in Russia and Eastern Europe in general has been fascinating, because it reminds me of how and why we were big in this country in 1972 and '73. For those countries the collapse of the Soviet bloc meant the end of a way of living and thinking, the transformation of a rigid, grey world a bit like the Britain I'd experienced as a kid and during the grim economic times of the early 1970s. Just as Slade was the right band back then for a country just getting colour televisions in big numbers, so we later brought colour to former communist countries emerging from their own black-and-white times. To also hear that they'd been smuggling our records in to listen to twenty years before, that really made me appreciate again just how important Slade had been.

And to still do big UK tours, to have so many people come out and see us, some who saw us the first time around and some who are new fans, that has been really encouraging. I think what it's done is underline just how ingrained Slade is in British DNA. That sound, those songs, have become a part of people's lives, and the Christmas song is as much a part of that time of year as Christmas trees, the Queen's speech and *A Christmas Carol*.

It's all helped my self-confidence too, and I now spend more time writing material and putting songs together at home than I ever did in the early days. I've become much more interested in creating, whereas in the past my sole focus was on performing. I've developed an interest in playing classical guitar too. Music is still very much the passion that fires me on a daily basis.

So that's the end of the book, but it's not the end of the story. I'm still looking forward to my next show. As long as I'm fit and able, and as long as I've got the enthusiasm that I still have as I write this, I'll be up there on stage, playing with Slade, entertaining people, trying to give them a good night out, hoping to give them the chance to escape into those songs from the cares of the world.

As well as the personal contentment I've found, I'm lucky that I do something that has value, that I love and that people want and enjoy. It's almost unbelievable, but it's still a thrill to go out on that stage and connect with an audience. I just hope there are plenty more gigs to come.

After all, after fifty years in Slade, what else can I do but look to the future...

AFTERWORD

No Slade = No Oasis. It's as devastating and as simple as that.

The Stone Roses? Yeah, they played their part.

The Beatles? Well they were undeniably great... but Slade? I felt their songs could've been written at the end of my street... in a house just like mine.

I loved them as a child in the 70s and I grew to love even more in the 90s.

Dave Hill? He was keeping it casual during The Glam Wars on *Top of the Pops* and he had a gold Rolls Royce!! Invented The Super Yob and wore a cape!!

What's not to love?

Noel Gallagher

ACKNOWLEDGEMENTS

Writing my autobiography has been a great way of meeting up and talking with many of the wonderful people who make my life so amazing. Some of these I'd not met or spoken to for decades. It's also taken me back to some incredible times and made me think of those who are no longer with us.

It's impossible to mention all these folks in my book, and indeed not all the stories could make it in here either. So, I'd like to thank a few very important people.

Firstly, my family. Thanks to my mom and dad for letting me be a free spirit and follow my dreams. Dad, who was also one of the biggest fans of Slade, not only let me do what I wanted but also fixed the band's van, ferried me about, looked after stray fans and very importantly bought me the Gibson guitar which I still play to this day and which defines the Slade sound.

Carol, who is just the best sister in the world, also came out with some cracking tales, a few which I'd never heard before.

To my cousin Gerald Whitehouse, who I'd not seen for over forty years, a big thank you for revealing a very interesting story about Mom and Dad.

I can never thank my wife Jan enough, she is my rock, my everything, and has been a tremendous help with putting my book together. To my kids, Jade, Sam, Bibi and my grandkids, Macy, Roman, Jacob, Alfie and Savannah, you mean everything to me.

I also had a great insight about Mom and Dad from our old neighbours – the Woolleys – Roger, Susan and Brenda. Lovely people and it's great that we're still in touch some sixty-odd years later.

To Tony, my school mate, partner in crime and first bass player, thanks for the wonderful crazy times. Evo – Wolverhampton's very own 'Cliff Richard' – not only reminded me of some great times, which I'd forgotten about, but also brought the swinging 60s and lively local music scene back to life for me.

To Slade, past and present, I am thankful to Don, Nod and Jim for your contributions to my life and the fun we had together, the commitment we had to be the best band that we could be. I would also like to thank John, Mal, Robin, Tim, Susanne and the much missed Swinn, who sadly passed away only a few weeks after I interviewed him for this book. To the legions of roadies, technicians, engineers, producers, pluggers, DJs, promoters, journalists, photographers, record-company and record-shop people, a huge thank you.

Just as I am writing this, I hear that Roger Allan has passed away. He was called the 'Brian Epstein of Wolverhampton'. He was a great help with our first record deal, for Ambrose Slade's *Beginnings*. Our manger-to-be, Chas Chandler, heard that LP and then sought us out. And, as they say, the rest is history.

Thanks to Steve and Barbara Megson who put together many of the amazing and crazy outfits for me in the 1970s. I'm sure that they must have kept the silver paint business buoyant for years!

Keith Altham was Slade's inventive publicist extraordinaire and I still very much appreciate his friendship and wisdom.

At the 'business end' of Slade there's accountant Colin Newman and lawyer Nick Kanaar who are the safest and most trusted hands you could ask for.

I've had – and have – some of the best managers in the business. Without a doubt Chas Chandler played a pivotal role in Slade's success. The next manager I had was Len Tuckey. I would like to say a big thank you to Len who helped focus and convince me to go back on the road as Slade. Taking care of me and Slade now is Abbie Carter, the late Hal Carter's daughter. She is much more than just a great manager. I would like to thank her greatly for the fantastic job she does and continues to do.

Outside of Slade, Wizzard's keyboardist Bill Hunt has been one of my main writing and creative partners and my thanks go to him. Also, thanks to John Diggins for creating my latest guitar.

Dr Lisa Brownell, thank you for helping me through the dark times.

I would also like to thank Mike Bell, the late Andy Matthews, Jude Aflalo, Mike Read, Matthew Patten, Emma Lewendon, Marc Michalski and Jamie Masters for all their hard work on the *Slade Live at Koko's* DVD.

There are a lot of publishers out there, but I've been very lucky to find the perfect one for me at Unbound. It's been a genuine pleasure working with the talented and passionate team there, but a special thank you goes to John, Amy, Georgia, Phil and Anna. I also worked closely with Wednesbury's finest Dave Bowler who helped get my story down on paper and made sense of some of my crazy mad stories!

Many thanks to Slade historian Chris Selby for his help tracking down photographs.

Without the help, guidance and talents of Anthony Keates this book would not be in your hands. A local lad from Walsall, a Slade fan and my right-hand man, he also shares my love of pork pies.

Thank you to all the Slade fans. You are the reason that in my seventies, I am still rocking the world with Slade. I hope to see you soon!

My final thank you goes to my mom. Firstly for bringing me into the world, gving me her smile and allowing me to be what I wanted to be, and then to my much-loved grandfather, David Bibby, from whom I surely inherited my passion and talent for music.

INDEX

Lincoln Festival, 118, 124, 179
Little Richard, 100
Love Affair, 85
Lynn, Vera, 205
Lynne, Jeff, 99

McCartney, Paul, 30, 41, 48
McNulty, Mal, 226, 228, 230
Madame Tussaud's, 115
Makin, Steve, 194, 228, 230
Mallin, Ken, 57, 62–3
Malpas, Mrs, 14
Mander Centre, Wolverhampton, 109
Mankowitz, Gered, 84, 123–4
marijuana (pot), 63, 75, 124, 168
Marston, Mick, 37, 44, 47, 49–50
Martin, Irving, 71
Marvin, Hank, 35, 40, 42
Matthew, Brian, 41
Mavericks, the, 88
Mayall, John, 56
Memphis Cutouts, 48
Mercury, Freddie, 104
Middle of the Road, 105
Midlands Today, 148
Midnight Special, 166
Mildmay of Flete, Lord, 4
Miller, Glenn, 243
Miller, Max, 104
Mitchell, Joni, 168
Money, Zoot, 48, 102
Monsters of Rock festival, 183
Montgomery, Wes, 29
Morris, Angela, 89, 130–1, 133–4
Most, Mickie, 81
Mott the Hoople, 99, 104
Move, the, 98
MTV, 185
Mud, 159

'N Betweens, the, 39, 42–3, 47, 49, 53, 72
New Seekers, 105
Nick and the Axemen, 48
Nicky Nacky Noo, 72
Nugent, Ted, 75

Oh Boy!, 31
Oldham, Andrew Loog, 80
Olympic Studios, 107
One Flew Over the Cuckoo's Nest, 16
Osbourne, Ozzy, 177, 185, 194, 248
Osbourne, Sharon, 185–6
Osmond, Donny, 149–50

Page, Jimmy, 12, 16
Pan's People, 111, 132
Peel, John, 102
Performance, 156
Perrin, Les, 198
Pink Floyd, 75, 248
platform soles, 104, 120, 128, 165, 170
Polydor, 103, 108–9, 137, 143, 147, 174, 189–91
Porter, Cole, 128
Powell, Don
  and band break-up, 187–95
  and band difficulties, 175–7
  car accident, 130–4
  clothes and appearance, 93
  and 'Coz I Luv You', 106
  and Dave's health, 226–7
  drumming style, 133
  early years, 41, 43–4, 46–7
  filming *Flame*, 155, 159
  forms Slade, 48–52
  house buying, 141
  and 'Merry Xmas Everybody'

SUPPORTERS

Unbound is a new kind of publishing house. Our books are funded directly by readers. This was a very popular idea during the late eighteenth and early nineteenth centuries. Now we have revived it for the internet age. It allows authors to write the books they really want to write and readers to support the books they would most like to see published.

The names listed below are of readers who have pledged their support and made this book happen. If you'd like to join them, visit www.unbound.com.

Frode Aanonsen
Vidar Aas
Robert Abel
Gary Abraham
Stefan Ahlstrom
Philip Ali
Andy Allen
Richard Allen
Lulu Allison
Michael Ambeau
Randy America
David Annand
Carole Archer
Chris Archer

Shaun Ashcroft
Dave Avery
Martin Baeckerling
Jason Baker
John Baker
Martin Baker
Peter Baker
Paul Bamford
Andy Banham
Bob Bankhead
Ray Banks
John Barker
Steven Barker
David Barraclough

David Bateman
Jonathon Bebbington
Phil Beddow
Martin Beeson
John Belam
Marnik Ace Bellecoste
David Bennett
Bernard
John Berry
Stephen Bevis
Daren Bishop
Stephen Blickett
Daniel Bloomfield
Lenny Bobbio
Andy Boden
Bones
Dave Bradley
Tommy Brannigan
Robert Brewer
David Bridge
Ivan Brighty
John Briscoe
Andy Brookes
Jonathan Brown
Paul Brown
Stephen Brunsdon
Keith Brunt
Pete Bryden
Timothy Buckeridge
Martin Bundy
Jacqueline Bunt
Richard Bunting
Anthony Burlton
Steve Bustard
Marcus Butcher
Neil Cadman
Bruce Campbell
Graham Campbell
Mark Campbell
Andrew Campling
Andrew Carpenter

Julie Carter
Julian Cartwright
Frank Casale
Peter Casey
Barry Casterton
Mark Cawdery
Steven Chalmers
Mick Chapman
Juan Christian
Leigh Clark
Steve Cobbett
Alan Cockayne
Malcolm Coghill
Chris Coles
John Collett
Tim Collett
Claudie Combelas
Steve Comer
Jennie Condell
Daragh Connolly
Stephen Copson
Paul Corfield
Katy Costello
Richard Cox
Cheryl Coxall
James Craig
Nigel Craig
John Cullen
John Cutler
Mark Cutler
Tim Daines
Sharon Dale
John Dalton
Michael Damkvist
Steve Dandy
Martyn Daniel
Elizabeth Darracott
Charles Darrow
Phillip Dascombe
Les Davidson
Paul Davidson

Bill Davies
Jeff Davies
David M. Davison
Garry Daws
Marc Debouver
Hendrik Dedeurwaerder
Paul Delaney
Richard Denham
Pierre Deweerdt
Mick Dickinson
Eef Diepenbroek
Andrew Dodd
Norman Donohue
Ron Dovey
John Drake
Peter Duerden
Stephen Duffy
Tim Duffy
Graham Dumble
Stephen Durrans
Mark Dyer
Mark Eagling
Phil Edginton
Alan Edmunds
Ian Edmundson
Paul Edwards
Steve Edwards
John F. Eggerman
Tim Elford
Thomas Enbäck
Bjorn Ertesvag
Jan Ertesvag
Andrew Ettle
Matthew Evans
Sian Evans
Julie Evans-Mulligan
Kelly Falconer
Alan & Susan Fantom
David Farmer
Andrew Faulkner
David Fearn

Pete Fender
Michael Fickel
Emma Fili
Trevor Fillingham
Andy Flemmings
Andrew Flux
Andrew Forcer
Nick Fordy
Nigel Fowler
Aldo Framingo
Adrian Francis
Bob Freeman
Uwe Friedrich
Rainer Frilund
Samuel Furingsten
Ludwig Fuss
Rob Gadsby
Austin Gannon
John Garland
Nicholas George
Claire Gibbons
Steve Gibson
William Gilbert
Henry Giles
Alan Gill
Sukie Gladstone
Adam Glover
Laurence Glover
Paul Glover
Susan Godfrey
John Goldfinch
Kev Golding
Paul Goverd
Lennart Grääs
Jonas Granath
Mark Gray
Martin D Green
Colin Slade Grimshaw
Tony Grist
John Groat
Franz Gruber

Dave Guerin
Shane Hadley
Ian Hall
George Hannah
James Hannington
Michel Harperath
Philip Harris
Star Harris
Nigel Hart
Ian Hartley
Martin Haslam
Peter Hawkins
Richard Hawkins
Rebecca Haywood
Frank Healy
Phil Heath
Paul Henderson
William Henderson
Martin Hepplestone
Julie Hepplestone(Willis)
Louise Hewitt-Wall
Robert Hextall
Christopher Hickling
Paul Higham
Ian Hill With Love On Your
   Birthday x Jo x
Johan Hillbom
Jon Hobbs
Paul Hodcroft
Kelvin Hoggett-Thompson
Anders Holmberg
Jörgen Holmstedt
Chris Horseman
Paul Frederick Hoult
John Howarth
Lesley Hoyles
Martin Hughes
Barry Hulme
Miles Hunt
Russ Hunt
Metin Huseyin

Lynne Hush
Jostein Hustveit
Peter Hutchison
John & Judith Ireland
Tatsuya Ishii
Kay Jackson
Mick Jackson
Gert Jensen
Henrik Jensen
Per Jensen
Simon Jerrome
Colin Jessop
Dave Jewell
Chris Johnson
Derek Paul Johnson
John Johnson
Andrew Jones
Kevin Jones
Mike Jones
Stephanie Jones
Trevor Jammy Jones
Wayne Jones
Keith Julian
KC/DC
Matt Toughsticks Kelly
David Kemp
Vikki Kennelly
Jonathan Kereve-Clarke
David Kerr
Dan Kieran
Michael Kierans
Vebjørn Kildehaug
Simon Kimmins
Dave Kinch
Andrew King
Ian King
Phil Kinrade
Steve Knibbs
Gerald Knight
Steve Knight
Ted Kniker

Valentine Kononenko
Joachim Kornmayer
Ralf Kotzur
Andrew Lacey
Julia Lamberton
Seppo Lampovaara
Brian Large
Mick Larkin
Colin Launder
David Law
Tristan Lawton
Garry Lay
Alan Layton
Dickey Lee
Brian Leek
Dainis Leinerts
Mark Lendich
Martin Lewis
Sarah Lewis
Steve Leys
Martin Lienau
Ronny Lindgren
Mark Lion
Stephen Locke
Luis Lopes
John Lund
Frieder Lutz
John Lyall
Alan MacLennan
David Maddocks
Maggie
Budge Magraw
Paul Mancini
Mark
Michael Marks
Steve Mars
Graham Marsh
Jean Marshall
Trevor Martin
Steven Martin-Styles
Steve Mason

Anne Mather
John Mathie
Marlies Matthews
Tim May
Andy Maybourn
Owen McConnell
Gary McCrindle
Beth McGowan
Simon McLean
Richard McMahon
Shirley and Ian McMullon
Martin McQuillan
Ross McVie
Marie Therese McWalter
Chris Medd
Medlock Ceramics
Vlad Meşco
Rob Metcalfe
Neil Mettam
Jan Michielsen
Ian Millar
Tony Millington
Deiter Mills
Rich Mills
Michelle Milnes
Roger Mitchell
John Mitchinson
Jim Moore
Steve Moore
Kevin Morpeth
Gaz Morph
Tom Morton
Andrew Moss
Daryl Moughanni
Bjørn Munthe
Malcolm Mussell
Markus Naegele
Carlo Navato
Slava Nekrasov
Andrew Newberry
Nick Newsum

Adrian Newth

Leon Nicolaisen

Nomis

Fern Noyce

Clive Nutter

Adam Nutting

Lars Nysether

Peter O'Brien

Liam O'Connell

Denzil O'Donnell

Ken O'Keefe

Andrew O'Leary

Mark O'Neill

Flemming Odvig

Sue Oldham

Teri Olins

Wayne Oliver

Paul Osborn

Kevin Paish

Bryn Paling

Rebecca Paolucci

Steph Parker

David Parks

Neil Partridge

John Patterson

Steve Payne

James Pegg

Mark Pemberton

Mick Penn

Mark Pennington

Nigel Pennington

Clifford Penton

Terence Peppin

Elizabeth Perry

Matthias Petersen

Jonas Pettersson

Stephen Phelps

Scott Phillips

David Pinder

Nathan Pionke

Graham Platt

Justin Pollard

Jean Power

Helen Louise Powney

Robert Pratt

Gary Price

Paul Price

Alex Pritsker

Ilkka Pulliainen

Stephen Purdy

Adrian Purser

Tony Pye

Gary Pyke

Brent Quigley

Richard Ramage

Stuart Ramage

Mark Randall

Henri Rantanen

John Reddy

Phil Reed

Steven Reid

Mark Reynolds

Simon Reynolds

Chris Roberts

Wyn Roberts

Ken Robertson

Astrid Robson

Andrus Roes

Alan Roffey

Kim Rogers

Steve Rognas

Michael Rooker

Volker Rosenau

Stephen Rosevear

Garry Ross

Chris Rowsell

Michael Rozyla

Martin Ruston

Jane Sales

Scott Samuels

Carsten Scholz

Rudolf Schubert

Norbert Schwarz
Chris Selby
Nigel Self
Paul Sellers
Don Shaw
Harry Shaw Sr.
Mark Sheldon
David Shell
Katsumi Shiji
Fran Skellington
Malcolm Skellington
Trevor Slaughter
Angus Smart
Robert Smit
Alan Gary Smith
Ashley Smith
Duncan Smith
John Smith
Mark Smith
MTA Smith
Neil Smith
Peter Smith
Sharkey Smith
Steven Smith
Stewart Smith
Tony Smith
Paul Smyth
Vladimir Sokolov
Zdeněk Šotola
Steve Speed
Duncan Spokes
Andre St-Amand
Jeff Stacey
Doug Stafford
Peter Stead
Terry Stevens
Mick Stevenson
Andy Stewart
William Stewart
David Stimpson
Tabatha Stirling

Craigie Storey
Martin Ström
Niels Strufe
Åke Svensk
John Swanner
Dominic Symington
Stuart Tait
Joe Tasker
Derek Tate
Alan Taylor
Alun Taylor
Michael Taylor
David Taylor & Mr Peanut
Tim Tearle
Kevin Teece
Liam Telling
Alan Tennie
Denver Thirlwell
Laura Thompson
Paul Thompson
Bill Thomson
Mike Thorn
David Tinkham
Brian Titley
Morten Tolg
Steve Tomalin
Morten Torp
Mary Trapp
Brian Treanor
Tania Trimble
David G Tubby
Alan Tucker
Michelle Tuft-Smith
Mark Francis Tully
Andrew Turner
Boris Tuzov
Nigel Tyers
John Eivind Ullenes
Gerry Usher
Michael Van Overstraeten
Francis Vandewalle

Craig Vaughton
Arvid Vikse
Leif Haavard Vikshaaland
Anders Wååg
Nick Waite
David Walker
Steve Walker
Max Wall
Alistair Wallace
Friz Wallace
Kathryn Warner
Gerald Watson
Mark Welch
Paul Welsby
Trevor West
David Westbury
Lars-Erik Westby
Steve Weston
Nigel White

Michael Wilkins
Mick Wilkinson
Andy Williams
Lorna Williams
Trevor Williams
Jane Willis
Stevie J Wilson
Clive Wisbey
Greg Woolliscroft
Hayley Worstencroft
Glenn Worth
Chris Wray
Jon Wright
Marcus Wright
Tim Wright
Weston Wright
Penny York
Mary Bridget Young
Ady Zeimet

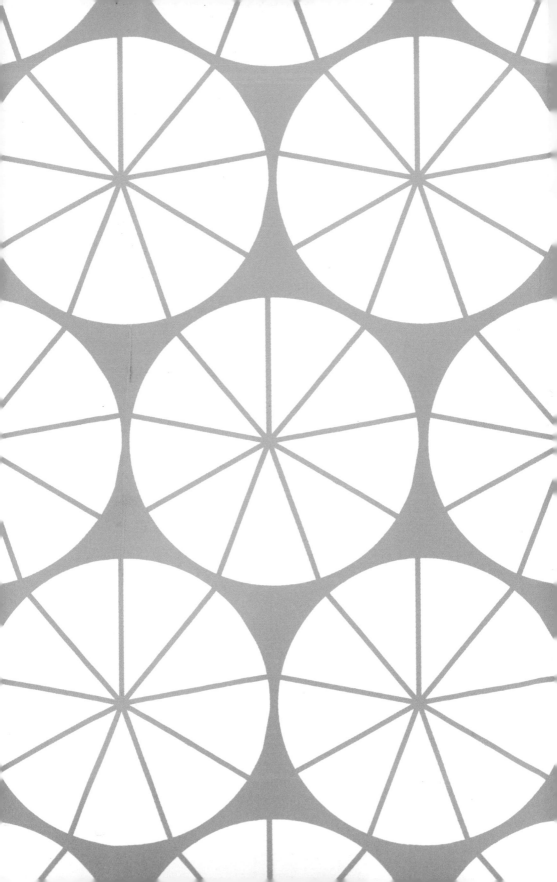